KNITTING
sensational
STITCHES

Lyric Books Limited

© 1994 Lyric Books Limited,
7-8 Ritz Parade, Western Avenue, London W5 3RA, England

First published 1994

ISBN 0 7111 0083 7

Printed in Belgium by
Proost International Book Production

Series Consultant: Eleanor Van Zandt
Art Editor: Stefanie Paradine
Graphics: Pauline Moss
Production Editor: Monika York

CONTENTS

Introduction

This book, the third in the STITCHES series, offers you a wealth of ideas for giving your knitting decorative appeal. There are special tips for working lace patterns and step-by-step instructions for working bobbles, for knitting with beads and sequins and for creating smocked fabrics. We have also included the knitter's 'star turn': the trellis (entrelacs) pattern. There are instructions for basic crochet, fringe, cords, tassels and some of the most popular embroidery stitches, all techniques that you can employ on occasion to give your knitted garments an extra flourish.

To tempt you to knit something glamorous we have provided two lacy sweaters, a long slinky one for evening and a crisp cool one with cable and bobbles for a summer day, a sensuous mohair sweater with a richly textured cable design, a sleeveless evening top embellished with beads, an elegant ribbed cardigan with appliqué, and a short cabled top with deep lace edging.

Among the stitches you'll find dozens of lace patterns from small and subtle to big and spectacular and a selection of edgings, bobbles, cables and fancy ribs, which you can use on a plain stocking stitch sweater to give it your own touch of style.

LACE KNITTING

Lace knitting can be used in many different ways - as an all-over pattern, as a horizontal or vertical panel or as single or random motifs. As a general rule, lace stitch patterns are most effective when worked in smooth yarns which show the detail of the pattern most clearly, although some patterns work well in mohair and angora mixes. Finer yarns are more suitable than bulky ones, as they give the stitches a more delicate appearance. Lace knitting is especially popular for baby garments.

Lace stitch patterns are produced by using the eyelet methods of increasing. The eyelet is usually worked in conjunction with a decrease so that the number of stitches remains constant at the end of each row. However, some of the most beautiful lace effects are achieved by increasing stitches on one or more rows and decreasing the extra stitches on subsequent rows. Circular shawls are produced by continually increasing stitches on every round (or every alternate round) while working the increases into the lace pattern.

Knitting lace is often considered to be 'for experts only' but there are simple lace patterns as well as complex ones. A small pattern repeat can be quite easy to follow and four, six or eight rows soon become familiar. (Usually only the right side rows are patterned - the wrong side rows are purled). However, large pattern repeats consisting of 24 rows or more require considerably more concentration.

Keeping a lace pattern correct

Complications often arise when a lace-patterned garment is shaped at the side edges - for example, when decreasing for the armhole or increasing along a sleeve edge. Unless row-by-row instructions are given the knitter will have to use skill and judgement to keep the lace pattern correct. The following rules should help.

Most lace patterns rely on the fact that for every eyelet or hole made, there is also a decrease. When shaping you should regard these as pairs and not work an eyelet without having enough stitches to work the decrease, and vice versa. Check at the end of every row that you have the correct number of stitches and that the eyelets and decreases are in the correct place above the previous pattern row. If there are not enough stitches to work both the eyelet and the decrease, work the few stitches at either end in the background stitch (usually stocking stitch). When only a few stitches are to be decreased - say at an armhole or neck edge - insert a marker at the end of the first pattern repeat in from the edge. At the end of every decrease row check that there is the correct number of stitches between the marker and the shaped edge. In some cases there may be only a partial repeat at the edge before shaping. The basic principle is to mark off a known unit of stitches and to count these while decreasing; in this way you avoid having to count the whole row.

If you are shaping over many rows, for example at a raglan edge, you may find that drawing the pattern and shaping on graph paper helps. This will tell you how to keep the pattern correct and also whether there are enough stitches left at the edge to work a complete repeat. Use the appropriate symbols given on pages 18 and 19 to chart the lace pattern.

Single cast-on

If you are knitting a fine lace object such as a shawl, that has a plain edge, you may wish to use this method of casting on. It is a very simple method but getting the right tension requires a little practice. You may find it easier when working the first row to knit into the back of each loop.

1. Make a slip knot near the end of the yarn, hold the ball yarn in your left hand as shown and take the needle point under the yarn, as shown by the arrow.

2. Pull down on the yarn to tighten the loop around the needle.

Repeat steps 1 and 2 for the number of stitches required.

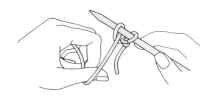

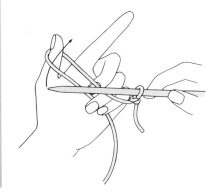

BOBBLES

Bobbles are used to create many interesting textured patterns. They can form an all-over pattern of regularly scattered bobbles or feature individually as accents, as in many Aran designs. They range in size from the smallest 'tuft' (or 'popcorn') to a large bobble that stands away from the background fabric.

Methods vary slightly but the basic

Types of Knitting

principle is always the same: a bobble is produced by creating extra stitches out of one original stitch or between two stitches. These stitches are then decreased immediately or on subsequent rows, or extra rows are worked on these stitches only before decreasing back to the original single stitch. Exact details of how to work a bobble are always given within pattern instructions but the following example shows a frequently used method.

Large bobble

Individual bobbles are produced by making three or more stitches out of the original one and then working extra rows over these stitches only. For an eye-catching effect these bobbles can be worked in a contrasting colour; or they can be worked in groups to form decorative clusters.

Bobbles can be worked in stocking stitch, reverse stocking stitch or garter stitch and usually consist of three, four or five stitches. The number of rows worked over the bobble stitches varies according to the size of bobble required.

The following instructions are for a large bobble worked in stocking stitch against a stocking stitch background and involve making five stitches out of one.

1. On a right side row knit to the position of the bobble. Knit into the front, back, front, back and front again of the next stitch, then slip the stitch off the left-hand needle so that five new stitches are on the right-hand needle instead of one.

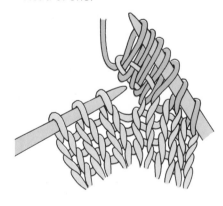

2. Turn the work so that the wrong side is facing and purl the five bobble stitches, then turn again and knit them. Repeat the last two rows once more,

thus making four rows in stocking stitch over the bobble stitches.

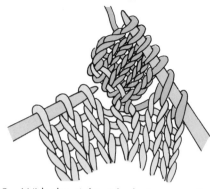

3. With the right side facing, use the left-hand needle point to lift the second, third, fourth and fifth bobble stitches, in that order, over the first one on the needle.

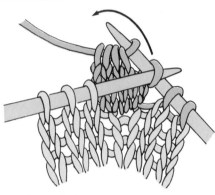

4. One stitch remains. Continue to work the rest of the row as instructed. Any small gap in the fabric will be hidden by the bobble.

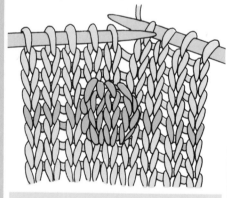

TIP

Allow plenty of extra yarn if you are adding bobbles to a plain fabric. If the bobbles are worked in a contrasting colour, use a separate length of the contrasting yarn for each bobble. When the bobble is completed, knot the two ends together and run them into the back of the bobble or along the wrong side of the work.

CABLES WITHOUT CABLE NEEDLES

A cable needle is not required for the simple action of transposing two stitches. The technique of crossing or twisting two stitches can be used to create a 'mock cable' in a vertical panel or to work a diagonal line of one raised stitch in stocking stitch on a stocking stitch or reverse stocking stitch background.

Crossing two stitches

Two stitches in stocking stitch can be crossed on every right side row either to the right or to the left. Working this in stocking stitch on a reverse stocking stitch fabric produces a decorative small mock cable.

Cross two stitches back

1. On a right side row, work to the position of the two-stitch cross. Miss the first stitch on the left-hand needle, and knit the second stitch, working through the front of the loop only. (This is easier if you first stretch the stitch a little with the point of the right-hand needle).

2. Do not slip the worked stitch off the needle but twist the needle back and knit the missed stitch through the front of the loop as usual. Then slip both stitches off the needle together.

This produces a stitch that crosses to the right and is called **Cross 2 Back (C2B)**.

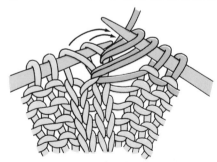

Purl these two stitches on the following

row. Repeat these two rows to produce a small mock cable twisting to the right.

Cross two stitches front

Work as given for C2B but knit the second stitch on the left-hand needle through the **back** of the loop, working behind the first stitch, then knit the first stitch in the usual way.

This produces a stitch that crosses to the left and is called **Cross 2 Front (C2F)**.

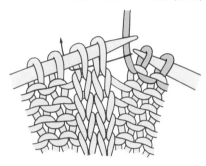

Twisting two stitches

The following techniques are used to make a diagonal line or 'travelling stitch' of one stitch in stocking stitch on a reverse stocking stitch background.

Twist two back

1. On a right side row, work to one stitch before the knit stitch. Miss the first stitch, then take the yarn back between the needles and knit the second stitch through the front of the loop.

2. Without slipping the worked stitch off the needle, purl the missed stitch through the front of the loop, then slip

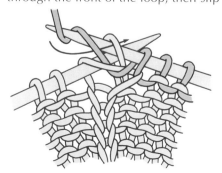

both stitches off the needle at the same time. This reverses the position of the two stitches and produces a line of knit stitches travelling to the right. It is called **Twist 2 Back (T2B)**.

Twist two front

1. On a right side row work to the knit stitch. Miss the knit stitch and purl the following stitch through the **back** of the loop, working behind the first stitch.

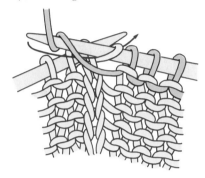

2. Without slipping the purled stitch off the needle, bring the needle to the front of the work and knit the missed stitch, then slip both stitches off the needle at the same time.

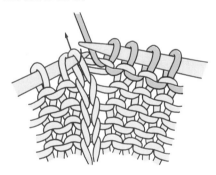

This produces a line of knit stitches travelling to the left. It is called **Twist 2 Front (T2F)**.

Because the technique is rather awkward to work you may find it easier to use a cable needle to hold the knit stitch at the front of the work.

CASTING OFF EDGES TOGETHER

If two sections to be seamed have the same number of stitches, they can be cast off together rather than sewn. This gives a very neat edge and can also save time. Leave the stitches on a spare needle at the end instead of casting them off, then use either of the following two methods to join the pieces together.

Method 1

Place the two pieces together with right sides together, then, using the same size needle as was used for the main part of the knitting, *knit together the first stitch from the front needle with the first stitch from the back needle. Repeat from the * once more (two stitches on the right-hand needle). Pass the first stitch over the second to cast it off. Continue in this way until all the stitches are cast off, then fasten off the last stitch in the usual way.

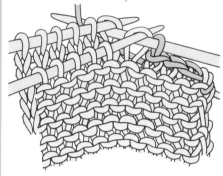

Method 2

Place the two pieces together with right sides facing, then, using the same size needle as was used for the main part of the garment, pull the first stitch on the back needle through the front stitch. Lift the stitch on the front needle over this stitch and off the needle. Continue in this way until all stitches are transferred to the right-hand needle. Slip the stitches back on to the left-hand needle, if necessary, and then cast the stitches off in the usual way.

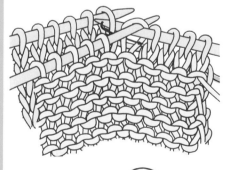

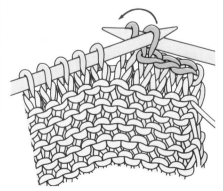

Types of Knitting

KNITTING WITH BEADS

Beads can be knitted into a garment in a random or evenly spaced design or incorporated into a lace or textured pattern. The background fabric should be fairly firm, or the beads may slip through to the wrong side. Also, the additional weight of the beads may tend to drag a loosely knitted garment out of shape, particularly if the yarn itself is quite heavy.

Choosing the correct beads for the design is very important. There is an enormous variety of beads available in all shapes, sizes and materials, such as plastic, wood, 'pearl', metal and glass. You must make sure that the beads chosen are a suitable weight for the yarn and style of garment and that they have a large enough hole for the yarn to pass through. Test your beads by adding them to your tension swatch - if they are too heavy the knitting will sag.

Beads are generally knitted into a fabric using a ball of yarn on to which they have been threaded before the work commences. For the knitting use one of the methods given below, according to the pattern instructions or your own choice. These methods give slightly different end results, so try a small swatch before deciding which method you prefer.

Threading beads

You will need a sewing needle and thread to transfer the beads on to the yarn. Most patterns specify the number of beads to be threaded on to each ball of yarn. If this information is not available thread up one ball with more beads than you think you will need, then count the number used after completing that ball of yarn. It is important to thread the correct number of beads (or more) on to the yarn before beginning to knit; once the ball is started you will not be able to add any more unless you thread them from the other end of the yarn or break the yarn to make a new length.

1. Check that the needle will pass through the beads. Cut a length of thread about 15 cm [6 ins] long and thread both ends into the needle, thus forming a loop of thread at one end.

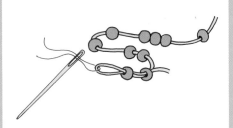

Pass one end of the knitting yarn through the loop of sewing thread. Hold the end of yarn in place, then slip the beads down the needle, along the thread and over the doubled yarn.

Adding beads from the back

Method 1

In this technique the beads are added as you work a wrong side row and are pushed through to the right side. They are held in place within the fabric and always lie at a slight angle.

1. On a wrong side row, work to the position of the beaded stitch. Insert the right-hand needle purlwise into the next stitch, wind the yarn around the needle and slide a bead down the yarn so that it is touching the needle.

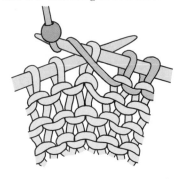

2. Purl the stitch, using your left thumb to push the bead through the stitch and on to the right side of the work.

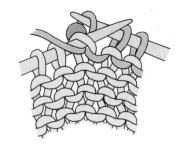

3. Secure the bead at the front on the following right side row by knitting into the **back** of the beaded stitch. Use your

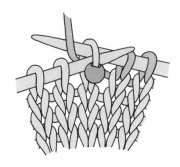

left thumb to hold the bead in position as you knit the following stitch.

Method 2

In this method the beads are also added on a wrong side row but they lie horizontally to the front of the fabric on the loop between two knit stitches.

On a wrong side row work to the stitch before the position of the bead. Knit the next stitch, slide the bead along the yarn up to the stitch just worked, knit the next stitch, then work the following stitches as instructed. It is important that the stitches at either side of the bead be **knitted** (regardless of the stitch pattern being worked) to ensure that the bead lies at the front of the fabric.

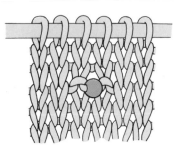

Adding beads with a slip stitch

Perfect for a lightly sprinkled surface, these beads 'hang' very slightly from the strand of the slipped stitch on the surface of the fabric.

1. On a right side row, work to the position of the beaded stitch. Bring the yarn forward to the front of the work and push a bead down the yarn so that it lies against the needle at the front of the work.

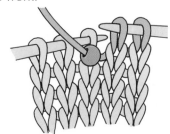

handwritten: FOR DRESS
WORK PATTERN to ARMHOLE, ADD ANOTHER 20R, to 16"
DECREASE 1 ST AT BACK END NEXT & ALT ROW to 109 STS (...)
SWITCH TO SMALLER NEEDLES FOR WAIST
3WELL-20R (2") then reincrease
to 109 rev 9 Dec + continue to Shape Dirmhole (20R)

Beaded Top

2. Slip the next stitch purlwise, leaving the bead in front of the slipped stitch. Take the yarn to the back and continue to work as normal.

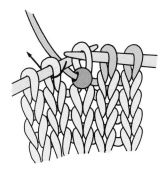

All-over bead knitting

This method is used to cover the knitted fabric entirely with beads so that the knitted stitches are not visible from the right side. This type of knitting was widely used in the 19th century, especially for making purses in which decorative patterns were formed by threading different coloured beads in a particular order. Obviously, this type of knitting is very time consuming, but for a small item, such as an evening bag, the results can be well worth the effort.

It is preferable to use a strong, fine yarn for this and to work with a firm tension. Because so many beads are required - one for every stitch - it is easier to wind the yarn into several smaller balls before threading. Work in stocking stitch but work into the **back** of every stitch on both knit and purl rows. On knit rows, push the bead up to the needle and knit the stitch through the back of the loop, making the new loop large enough to be able to pull the bead through to the right side. On purl rows the bead automatically lies on the right side of the fabric. Always join in the new lengths of yarn at the beginning of a row, never in the middle.

Measurements

		75/80	85/90	95/100	cm
To fit bust size		30/32	34/36	38/40	ins
Finished measurement		85	95	105	cm
		34	38	42	ins
Length to shoulder		54	56	58	cm
		21¼	22	23	ins

Shown in 75/80 cm [30/32 inch] size.

Materials

4 ply knitting yarn		200	250	300	grams
		8	9	11	ounces

Pair needles each size 3¼mm (UK 10, USA 3 or 4) and 2¾mm (UK 12, USA 2). 86(92-92) beads.

The quantities of yarn stated are based on average requirements and are therefore approximate.

For abbreviations see pages 18 and 19.

Tension

28 sts and 36 rows = 10 cm [4 ins] square measured over st st using larger needles.

Special Abbreviation

Bead 1 = yf, push a bead up close to work, sl 1 purlwise, yb.

Threading Beads

You will require a sewing needle and thread to transfer the beads on to the yarn. Thread the correct number of beads (or more) on to the yarn before commencing, as once the ball is started you will not be able to add any more unless it is done from the other end of the yarn, or by breaking the yarn.

TIP

Instead of knitting in beads you may prefer to sew them on to the completed fabric using transparent nylon thread.

Front

Using smaller needles cast on 111(125-139) sts.

1st row (right side): K1, *p1, k1; rep from * to end.

2nd row: P1, *k1, p1; rep from * to end.

Rep the last 2 rows until rib measures 9 cm [3½ ins] ending with a right side row. *handwritten:* 3INS (21 ROWS)

Next row (increase): Rib 6, *inc in next st, rib 13(15-17); rep from * to last 7 sts, inc in next st, rib to end. 119(133-147) sts.

Change to larger needles and work in st st starting with a knit row until front measures 33 cm [13 ins] ending with a purl row. *handwritten:* 80 R?

Shape Armholes

Cast off 4(5-6) sts at beg of next 2 rows. Dec 1 st at each end of next 5 rows, then every following alt row until 97(107-119) sts remain ★. Work straight until armholes measure 8(9-11) cm [3(3½-4¼) ins] from start of armhole shaping ending with a purl row. *handwritten:* 22R

Commence beading.

1st row: K27(32-38), [Bead 1, k5] 7 times, Bead 1, k27(32-38).

Work 3 rows in st st starting with a purl row.

5th row: K24(29-35), [Bead 1, k5] 8 times, Bead 1, k24(29-35).

Work 3 rows in st st starting with a purl row.

9th row: K21(26-32), [Bead 1, k5] 9 times, Bead 1, k21(26-32).

Work 3 rows in st st starting with a purl row.

13th row: K18(23-29), [Bead 1, k5]

Beaded Top

10 times, Bead 1, k18(23-29).

Work 2 rows in st st starting with a purl row.

Shape Neck

1st row: P35(40-46), turn and complete this side first.

2nd row: K2tog, [k5, Bead 1] 3 times, k15(20-26).

Starting with a purl row, work 3 rows in st st decreasing 1 st at neck edge on each of these rows.

6th row: K2tog, k4, [Bead 1, k5] twice, Bead 1, k12(17-23).

Starting with a purl row, work 3 rows in st st decreasing 1 st at neck edge on 1st and 2nd of these rows.

10th row: K2tog, k4, [Bead 1, k5] twice, Bead 1, k9(14-20).

Starting with a purl row, work 3 rows in st st decreasing 1 st at neck edge on 2nd of these rows.

14th row: K2tog, [k5, Bead 1] 3 times, k6(11-17). 25(30-36) sts remain.

Continue beading.

Work 3 rows in st st starting with a purl row.

18th row: K3, [Bead 1, k5] twice, Bead 1, k9(14-20).

Work 3 rows in st st starting with a purl row.

22nd row: K6, [Bead 1, k5] twice, Bead 1, k6(11-17).

The last 8 rows set the bead pattern. Work 11(13-15) more rows in pattern thus ending with a purl row. Cast off.

With wrong side of work facing, slip next 27 sts on to a holder for neckband, rejoin yarn to next st and purl to end. 35(40-46) sts.

2nd row: K15(20-26), [Bead 1, k5] 3 times, k2tog.

Starting with a purl row work 3 rows in st st decreasing 1 st at neck edge on every row.

6th row: K12(17-23), [Bead 1, k5] twice, Bead 1, k4, k2tog.

Starting with a purl row work 3 rows in st st decreasing 1 st at neck edge on 1st and 2nd of these rows.

10th row: K9(14-20), [Bead 1, k5] twice, Bead 1, k4, k2tog.

Starting with a purl row work 3 rows in st st decreasing 1 st at neck edge on 2nd of these rows.

14th row: K6(11-17), [Bead 1, k5] 3 times, k2tog. 25(30-36) sts remain.

Continue beading.

Work 3 rows in st st starting with a purl row.

18th row: K9(14-20), [Bead 1, k5] twice, Bead 1, k3.

Work 3 rows in st st starting with a purl row.

22nd row: K6(11-17), [Bead 1, k5] twice, Bead 1, k6.

The last 8 rows set the bead pattern. Work 11(13-15) more rows in pattern thus ending with a purl row. Cast off.

Back

Work as given for Front to ★. Work straight until armholes measure 21(23-25) cm [8¼(9-10) ins] from start of armhole shaping ending with a purl row.

Shape Shoulders

Next row: Cast off 25(30-36) sts, knit until there are 47 sts on right-hand

needle, cast off remaining 25(30-36) sts.

Slip remaining sts on to a holder for the neckband.

Finishing and Bands

Block but do not press. Join left shoulder seam.

Neckband

Using smaller needles and with right side of work facing, knit across sts on holder at back neck decreasing 1 st at centre, pick up and k29(31-33) sts down left front slope, knit across sts on holder at front neck and pick up and k29(31-33) sts up right front slope. 131(135-139) sts.

Starting with the 2nd row, work 8 rows in rib as given for Front. Cast off in rib.

Join right shoulder seam and ends of neckband.

Armbands

Using smaller needles and with right side of work facing, pick up and k141(157-171) sts evenly around armhole edge.

Starting with a 2nd row, work 8 rows in rib as given for Front. Cast off in rib.

Join side seams and ends of armbands.

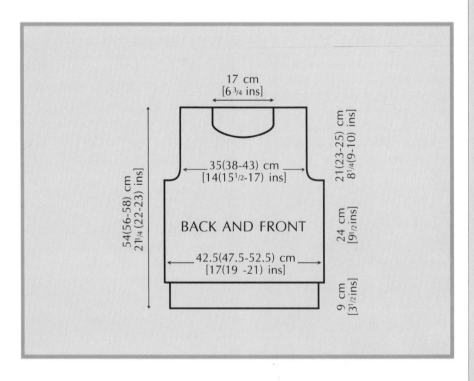

Types of Knitting

SMOCKING

There are two basic methods of smocking a piece of knitting: using a cable needle to smock the stitches while the work is in progress or using a sewing needle to embroider the smocking once the knitting is complete. Smocking is usually worked on a ribbed fabric, drawing together the knit stitches on the right side.

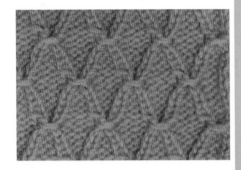

Cable needle method

This method is somewhat quicker than the embroidered method and involves slipping the stitches to be smocked on to a cable needle or double-pointed needle and winding the yarn around these stitches. The tension of the smocked fabric depends on the tightness of the yarn wound around the stitches and also on the number of rows worked between the rows of smocking.

For smocking worked on a k1, p3 rib pattern, work as follows:

Cast on a multiple of 8 sts plus 7 extra.

Special Abbreviation

Smock 5 = slip next 5 sts on to cable needle and hold at front of work, wind yarn twice around sts on cable needle in an anti-clockwise direction, then k1, p3, k1 from the cable needle.

1st row (right side): P1, k1, *p3, k1; rep from * to last st, p1.

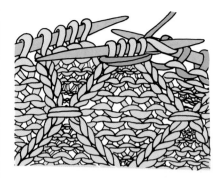

2nd row: K1, p1, *k3, p1; rep from * to last st, k1.

3rd row: P1, *Smock 5, p3; rep from * to last 6 sts, Smock 5, p1.

4th row: As 2nd row.

5th to 8th rows: Rep 1st and 2nd rows twice.

9th row: P1, k1, p3, *Smock 5, p3; rep from * to last 2 sts, k1, p1.

10th row: As 2nd row.

11th and 12th rows: As 1st and 2nd rows.

Rep these 12 rows.

This method creates a small gap in the work at either side of the smocked stitches. The technique can be adapted to any rib pattern provided the stitches on the cable needle begin and end with a knit stitch. The number of rows between the smocked stitches can also be varied as required.

It is possible to work the smocking in a contrasting colour; fasten this at the right-hand edge of the row to be smocked and strand it along the back of the knitting until needed.

Embroidery method

In this method the ribbed fabric is worked first and the smocking is applied to the completed fabric. The smocking can be worked either in the same yarn as the main fabric or in a contrasting yarn. The tension depends on how tightly the embroidery is worked and on how many rows there are between the smocked stitches.

Use a tapestry needle, which will pass easily between the stitches and work two backstitches through the work to draw the knit stitches together (see illustration). Count the number of rows between the smocking rows to make sure the smocking is worked evenly. If the ribs are widely spaced, you may

wish to fasten off each smocked stitch to avoid leaving long floats at the back of the work. This type of smocking can be applied to any ribbed fabric - the greater the distance between the knit stitches, the more pronounced the smocking will be.

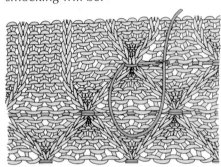

TRELLIS PATTERN

This is the name for an interwoven, criss-crossed fabric that is worked all in one piece. It is sometimes referred to by its French name, **Entrelacs**, which means 'interlaced design' . The pattern looks and sounds complicated, especially since the written instructions are so long, but the technique is relatively easy and soon becomes familiar once you start work.

The Large Trellis Pattern uses two colours in a way that is the basis of all versions of the stitch; the rectangles may vary in size, several colours may be used and textured or Fair Isle motifs can even be worked within each rectangle. In the following pattern the two colours are referred to as A and B. For abbreviations see pages 18 and 19.

Using A, cast on a multiple of 12 sts loosely (at least 24 sts).

Base Triangles: Using A, *p2 (wrong side of work), turn and k2, turn and p3, turn and k3, turn and p4, turn and k4, continue in this way working 1 more st on every wrong side row until the row 'turn and p12' has been worked; rep from * to end. Break off A.

1st row of Rectangles: Using B, k2, turn and p2, turn, inc in first st (by knitting into front and back of st), sl 1, k1, psso, turn and p3, turn, inc in first st, k1, sl 1, k1, psso, turn and p4, turn, inc in first st, k2, sl 1, k1, psso, turn and p5, turn, inc in first st, k3, sl 1, k1, psso, turn and p6, continue in this way working 1 more st on every right side row until the row 'inc in first st, k9, sl 1, k1, psso' has been worked (1 edge triangle complete), then continue as follows: *Pick up and k12 sts evenly along edge of next triangle, [turn and p12, turn and k11, sl 1, k1, psso] 12 times (1 rectangle complete); rep from * to edge of last triangle, pick up and k12 sts evenly along edge of last triangle, turn and p2tog, p10, turn and k11, turn and p2tog, p9, turn and k10, turn and p2tog, p8, turn and k9, continue in this way until the row 'turn and k2' has been worked, turn and p2tog (1 st remains on right-hand needle and edge triangle is complete). Break off B.

2nd row of Rectangles: Using A and continuing on from st on right-hand needle, pick up and p11 sts evenly along edge of triangle just worked, [turn and k12, turn and p11, p2tog] 12 times, then continue as follows: *Pick up and p12 sts evenly along side of next rectangle, [turn and k12, turn and p11, p2tog] 12 times; rep from * to end. Break off A.

3rd row of Rectangles: As 1st row but picking up sts along side edge of rectangles instead of triangles.

Rep 2nd and 3rd rows for pattern, ending with a 3rd row.

Final row of Triangles: Using A, *continuing on from st on right-hand needle, pick up and p11 sts evenly along edge of triangle just worked, turn and k12, turn and p2tog, p9, p2tog, turn and

---

k11, turn and p2tog, p8, p2tog, turn and k10, turn and p2tog, p7, p2tog, continue in this way working 1 st less on every wrong side row until the row 'turn and k3' has been worked. Turn and [p2tog] twice, turn and k2, turn and p1, p2tog, p1, turn and k3, turn and p3tog; rep from * but picking up sts along side of rectangle instead of triangle. Fasten off remaining st.

CROCHET ON KNITTING

Many knitted garments include a crochet edging or some other crocheted trimming. One of the commonest is a double crochet edging. (Note: American readers should substitute the word 'single' for 'double' in these instructions).

Double crochet edging

To work this edging use a crochet hook the same size or slightly smaller than the needles used for the knitting.

1. Hold the hook in the right hand and the yarn in the left hand as shown.

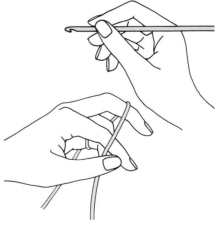

2. Insert the hook under the first stitch at one end from front to back, wind the yarn around the hook and draw a loop

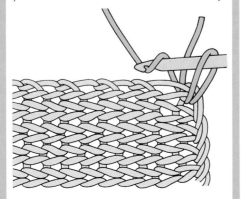

---

through from the back. Wind the ball yarn around the hook again and draw it through the loop on the hook. This joins the yarn to the fabric.

Pull the free end of the yarn tight; this can be darned into the work later.

3. Insert the hook one or two rows or stitches from the last point, draw through a loop from the back, then wind the yarn around the hook and draw it through the two loops on the hook (one double crochet worked).

Repeat step 3 as required to work a double crochet edging, checking that the edging is not so loose that it ripples or so tight that it distorts the fabric.

Button loop row

For a second row including chain stitch button loops, work as follows: Work one double crochet into every stitch of the previous row (and three stitches into each corner stitch). Work up to the position for the button loop. With one loop on the hook, *wind the yarn around the hook and draw through a new loop (one chain made). Repeat from the * until the required number of chain has been worked, then insert the hook into the appropriate stitch as instructed and continue in double crochet.

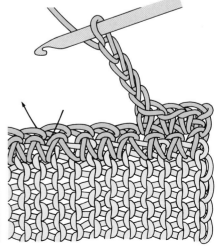

Finishing Touches

Casting off with a crochet hook

Using a crochet hook to cast off is not only extremely time-saving but useful when a loose, elastic cast-off edge is required, as you can gently loosen the stitch on the hook to ensure that the elasticity is retained.

To work this method use a crochet hook of the same size as the needles (or one size larger) and treat the crochet hook as if it were the right-hand needle. Knit or purl the first two stitches on to the crochet hook in the usual way. *Pull the second stitch through the first, knit or purl the next stitch and repeat from the * fastening off the last stitch in the usual way.

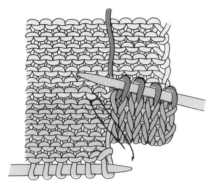

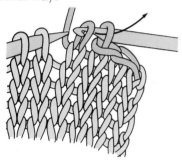

TUCKS

Tucks are best worked in fine yarn; they would be too bulky in a thick yarn as they contain two or three thicknesses of fabric.

Tuck worked across a row

For a tuck across an entire row work as follows:

Mark the last row before the start of the tuck with a contrasting thread at both edges. (In these illustrations the tuck itself is worked in a contrasting colour which simplifies the work). Work the required number of rows for the tuck, bearing in mind that the fabric will be folded in half, so twice the finished depth should be allowed; end with a wrong side row. Turn the work upside down and fold the tuck in half with wrong sides together so that the marked row is level with the base of the row on the needle. *Knit together the first stitch on the left-hand needle with the loop of the first stitch of the marked row; repeat from the * to the end of the row, matching the stitches from the marked row with the stitches on the left-hand needle.

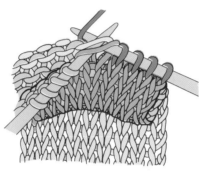

It may be easier to work the tuck if you first place the stitches from the marked row on a smaller size needle. The stitches can then be knitted together from the two needles.

Short tucks

Tucks can also be worked within the row to give a decorative puckered effect, as follows: *Work to the position for the tuck, turn the work upside down with wrong side facing, knit together the first stitch on the left-hand needle with the loop of the corresponding stitch on the chosen row above (depending on the thickness of the tuck); repeat from the * for the required width of the tuck, then work to the end of the row or the position of the next tuck.

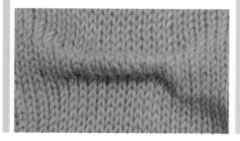

EMBROIDERY ON KNITTING

Embroidery stitches of various kinds can be used effectively to add an individual touch to a plain garment or complement a multi-coloured knitting design.

Stocking stitch garments make an ideal surface for embroidery, although it can also be added to lace patterns or cable panels. Embroidery is easier to work before the garment is sewn together. Whichever stitch you choose use a tapestry needle which has a blunt point which will not split the yarn. The yarn used for the embroidery should be approximately the same weight as that used for the knitting.

Swiss darning/duplicate stitch

This form of embroidery is used on a stocking stitch fabric. Each stitch covers an individual knit stitch - hence the alternative name 'duplicate stitch' - giving the appearance that the design has been knitted in. In addition to its use in working entire motifs, Swiss darning can also be used in conjunction with multi-coloured knitting - for example, to introduce a third colour to a row of Fair Isle knitted in two colours, to add a tiny area of colour to an intarsia design or to work very thin vertical or diagonal stripes in a plaid or diamond pattern.

Always match your tension to that of the knitting - too loose and the stitches will not be covered; too tight and the work will pucker. If the yarn used for embroidery is finer than the knitted yarn it may not cover the knitted stitch completely.

You can adapt small knitting or embroidery charts for Swiss darning. Note, however, that an embroidery chart will appear flatter when knitted because the width of a knitted stitch is greater than its height. For a more faithful interpretation buy some knitters' graph paper and re-chart the design using more rows to achieve the correct height.

Swiss darning horizontally

Work from right to left. Thread a tapestry needle with the embroidery yarn and weave in the yarn invisibly at the back of the work. Bring the needle out at the base of the first stitch, take it around the top of the stitch, then insert the needle back through the base of the same stitch, thus covering the original stitch completely. For the next stitch bring the needle through at the base of the next stitch to the left. Continue in this way until the appropriate stitches have been covered.

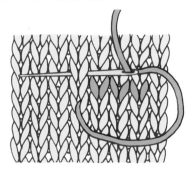

Swiss darning vertically

Work from bottom to top. Bring the needle out at the base of the first stitch, then take it around the top of the stitch. Insert the needle back through the base of the **same** stitch, then bring it up through the base of the stitch above, thus forming a vertical chain.

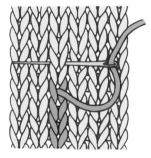

Other embroidery stitches

The following embroidery stitches are ideal for working on knitting. Designs can be simple - perhaps a simple cross stitch motif in one colour or a lazy daisy flower - or they can be much more elaborate using a combination of the stitches illustrated below in several colours. To keep the embroidery neat and uniform keep it in scale with the knitted stitches.

To prevent the fabric from moving while working fancy embroidery, draw the design on a piece of tissue paper and tack (baste) the paper to the knitting. Work the stitches through both paper and knitting, then remove the paper when the embroidery is complete. A pair of tweezers is useful in extracting stubborn bits of tissue.

Cross stitch

Work across one or two stitches and rows as required, inserting the needle between the stitches to avoid splitting the yarn. Take care to keep the slant uniform, with all the top stitches slanting either from lower left to upper right or vice versa, not a mixture of the two.

Chain stitch

This can be worked vertically, horizontally or diagonally across the fabric or in a curve.

Chain stitch using a crochet hook

This method can be used to work chain stitch vertically or diagonally across a knitted fabric where the stitches do not need to be duplicated as they do in Swiss darning. Fasten the yarn at the back, then insert the crochet hook through the first stitch from front to back and draw through a loop, insert the hook one or two stitches or rows from the original point (depending on the length of stitch required) and draw through another loop, then draw this through the loop on the hook to make a chain stitch on the right side of the fabric. Continue in this way for the required distance. To fasten off, cut the yarn and draw it through the last stitch, then weave the yarn in on the wrong side.

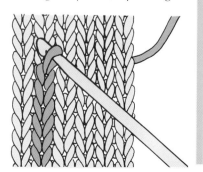

Stem stitch

This is a continuous line of long stitches worked from left to right. Each stitch overlaps the previous one by half its length.

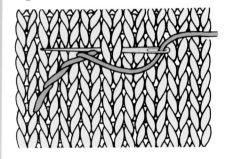

Satin stitch

This is used to cover an area of knitting with close parallel strands of thread. Practise it on a spare swatch of knitting until you get the tension right and can keep the edges smooth. First mark the area with backstitch, using a finer thread, then work the satin stitches over this outline.

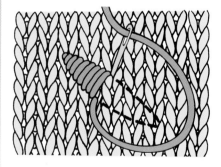

Lazy daisy stitch

This is a method of working individual chain stitches to form 'petals' which can be grouped together to make a 'flower' of four, five or more petals.

Finishing Touches

French knot

This stitch is often worked in the centre of a flower of lazy daisy stitches. Bring the needle up at the position for the knot and wind the yarn once or twice around the needle, according to the size of knot required. Take the needle back down close to the point where it emerged and draw the yarn through, thus forming a small knot on the right side.

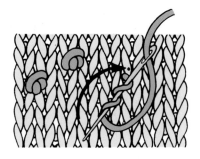

Blanket stitch

This stitch (also sometimes called 'buttonhole stitch') may be used along an edge where there is no ribbing - for example, around a neck edge. It can also be used in appliqué to finish the raw edge of a motif.

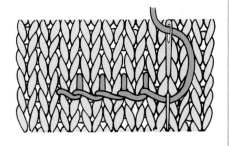

Appliqué

Appliqué can be used to decorate a plain garment and is frequently used in conjunction with embroidery and beading. Using a paper pattern, cut the required shape from fabric and interfacing. Tack (baste) the interfacing to the wrong side of the fabric and work

zigzag machine stitch around the edge. Pin or tack (baste) the motif in place and slip-stitch the motif to the garment using sewing thread and taking care not to distort the knitting. If you prefer you can work blanket stitch around the edge of the motif and through the knitted fabric at the same time.

TRIMMINGS

Knitted garments and accessories may be further embellished with various trimmings sewn or tied in place. Among the prettiest trimmings, suitable for lingerie, baby clothes and some evening clothes, are knitted edgings. A selection of these is given on pages 31 to 37. A variety of other trimmings is given here.

Fringing

Fringing is often worked along the edge of a scarf or shawl.

Simple fringe

Cut the required number of lengths for each group; the number of strands in each group determines the thickness of the fringe as well as the distance between each tassel. The strands should measure slightly more than twice the length of the finished fringe. Fold the strands in half and draw the folded end through the edge of the knitted fabric using a crochet hook. Draw the loose ends of yarn through the loop and pull them up firmly to form a knot. Trim the ends to neaten them.

Knotted fringe

With two or more rows of additional knots a fringe can be quite elegant. Fewer strands per group are required than for the simple fringe but they must be longer, about 13 cm [5 ins] is the minimum depth, so for this length cut the strands 27-28 cm [10½-11ins] long.

1. Knot the strands on to the edge of

the knitting as for a simple fringe.

2. On the next row knot together half the strands from each two adjacent groups. This will leave half a group free at each end.

3. On the next row knot half the strands from each two adjacent groups (those formed in step 2), thus bringing the outer strands into the pattern.

Add more rows of knots as required.

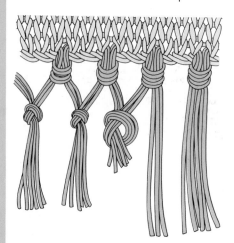

Looped fringe

This is a novel way of producing a fringed edging. The loops here are formed by unravelling knitted stitches from a band of garter stitches which is applied sideways to the garment edge.

1. Cast on enough stitches to give a border for sewing on plus stitches to unravel (about five or six stitches are usual; work a sample to determine the correct number). Work in garter stitch until the strip is the required length.

2. On the next row cast off only the stitches that form the border to be sewn to the garment. Cut off the yarn and fasten off. Slip the remaining stitches off the needle and unravel the rows individually to form loops.

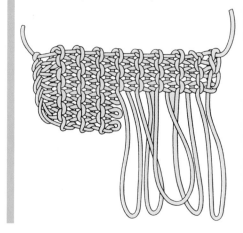

Tassels

Tassels are often used to decorate hats and novelty items.

1. Cut a rectangle of cardboard as wide as the length of the finished tassel. Wind the yarn around the cardboard until the required thickness is reached. Break the yarn, thread it through a sewing needle and pass the needle under all the loops. Do not remove the needle.

2. Tie the end of the yarn firmly around the loops, remove the card and cut through the loops at the end opposite the knot.

3. Wind the end of yarn around all the loops below the fold and fasten it securely. Pass the needle through the top and use the end to sew the tassel in place. Trim the ends neatly.

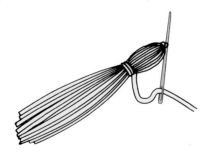

Pompons

Pompons are frequently used to decorate hats and may also be sewn together to make soft toys. They can be made in one colour or several and can vary in size from very tiny to quite large.

1. Decide on the size of the pompon, then cut two circles of cardboard with a diameter slightly bigger than the size of the finished pompon. Cut a smaller hole in the centre of each circle, about half the size of the original diameter. The larger this hole is, the fuller the pompon will be, but if you make it too large the pompon will be oval instead of round! To make sure that the holes are equal and aligned, cut one in one circle, then use the opening as a template for drawing and cutting the other.

2. Holding the two circles together, wind the yarn around the ring (using several strands at a time for speed) until the ring is completely covered. As the hole in the centre gets smaller you will need to use a tapestry needle to pass the yarn through.

3. Cut all around the yarn at the outside edge between the two circles using a pair of sharp scissors. Make sure that all the yarn has been cut.

4. Separate the two circles slightly, wind a length of yarn between them and tie it **firmly** in a knot, leaving an end long enough to sew the pompon in place. Pull the two circles apart and fluff out the pompon to cover the centre join. Trim around the ends of yarn to produce a smooth shape.

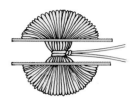

Twisted cords

Twisted cords are often used to thread through eyelet holes or as decoration on hats. They can be any length or thickness.

1. Cut the required number of strands of yarn about three times the length of the finished cord. For example, four strands of yarn 100 cm [40 ins] long will produce a cord eight strands thick and approximately 35 cm [14 ins] long. Knot the strands together at each end, making sure they are of equal length.

2. Attach one end to a hook or door handle and insert a knitting needle through the other. Turn the knitting needle clockwise until the strands are tightly twisted. The tighter the yarns are twisted, the firmer the finished cord will be. They should kink up the moment the tension is released.

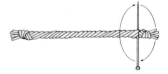

3. Holding the cord in the centre with one hand, bring both ends of the cord together allowing the two halves to twist together. Keep the cord fairly straight to avoid tangling and smooth it out evenly. Knot the cut ends together and trim them. Tie a knot in the folded end at the required point and cut the ends.

Abbreviations and Symbols

HOW TO READ STITCH CHARTS

Charts are read exactly as the knitting is worked, from the bottom to the top. After the last row at the top has been worked, repeat the sequence from row 1 unless otherwise stated. Each symbol represents an instruction. Symbols have been designed to resemble the actual appearance of the knitting.

Before starting to knit, look up all the symbols on your chosen chart so that you are familiar with the techniques involved. **Make sure you understand the difference between working similar symbols on a right side row and a wrong side row.**

Each square represents a stitch and each horizontal line a row. Place a ruler above the line you are working. If you are new to chart reading try comparing the charted instructions with the written ones.

Right Side and Wrong Side Rows

A 'right side row' is one in which the right side is facing you as you work and a 'wrong side row' is one in which the wrong side is facing as you work. Row numbers are shown at the side of the charts **at the beginning of the row.** Right side rows are always read from right to left. Wrong side rows are always read from left to right.

Symbols on the charts are shown as they appear from the right side of the work. Therefore, a horizontal dash stands for a purl 'bump' on the right side regardless of whether it was achieved by purling on a right side row or knitting on a wrong side row. To make things clearer, symbols on right side rows are slightly darker than on wrong side rows.

Pattern Repeats and Multiples

In charted instructions the pattern repeat is contained between heavier vertical lines. The extra stitches not included in the pattern repeat are there to 'balance' the row or make it symmetrical and are worked only once.

Panels

Panels are worked over a given number of stitches (not necessarily repeated).

All the panels in this book have been worked on a suggested background stitch. On the charts this is indicated by two stitches at either side of the panel. To work any of the panels you must cast on enough stitches to work the panel plus the required number of background stitches on each side.

Working from a Pattern

Instructions are given for the smallest size; larger sizes are given in ( )s. Figures or instructions given in [ ]s should be repeated as stated after the brackets. Where only one figure is given this applies to all sizes.

Stitch Pattern Multiples

The multiple or repeat of each stitch pattern plus the number of stitches needed to 'balance' the row is given with the written instructions.

To make working from the written instructions easier, in some instances one extra repeat has been added to the balancing stitches; THESE EXTRA STITCHES ARE NOT NEEDED ON THE CHARTS.

For American Readers

English terms are used in this book. Note the equivalent American terms:

Tension - Gauge

Cast Off - Bind Off

Stocking Stitch - Stockinette Stitch

Yf, Yfrn, Yon and **Yrn** (to make a st)- Yarn Over

Double Crochet - Single Crochet

Abbreviations and Symbols

The following abbreviations and symbols include all those used in this book.

Alt = alternate; **beg** = beginning; **ch** = chain; **cm** = centimetre(s); **dc** = double crochet; **dec** = decrease; **inc** = increase; **ins** = inches; **k** = knit; **KB1** = knit into back of stitch; **m** = metre(s); **mm** = millimetre(s); **p** = purl; **PB1** = purl into back of stitch; **psso** = pass slipped stitch over; **p2sso** = pass 2 slipped stitches over; **p3sso** = pass 3 slipped stitches over; **rep** = repeat; **sl** = slip; **sl st** = slip stitch; **st(s)** = stitch(es); **st st** = stocking stitch (1 row knit, 1 row purl); **tog** = together; **tbl** through back of loops; **yb** = yarn back; **yf** = yarn forward; **yfrn** = yarn forward and round needle; **yon** = yarn over needle; **yrn** = yarn round needle.

Inc 1 (Inc 1K or Inc 1P) = Increase 1 st knitwise or purlwise by knitting or purling into front and back of next st.

Note: Symbols are dark on right side rows and light on wrong side rows.

M1 (M1K [o] **or M1P** [o] **) = Make 1 st knitwise or purlwise** by picking up strand of yarn lying between last st worked and next st and knitting or purling into back of it.

I	**K** knit on right side rows
−	**K** knit on wrong side rows
−	**P** purl on right side rows
I	**P** purl on wrong side rows
S	**sl 1** slip one stitch purlwise with yarn at back of work, on right side rows.
S	**sl 1** slip one stitch purlwise with yarn at front (wrong side) of work, on wrong side rows.
V	**k1, p1, k1** into next stitch on right side rows
V	**KB1** knit into back of st on right side rows
<	**KB1** knit into back of st on wrong side rows
<	**PB1** purl into back of st on right side rows
V	**PB1** purl into back of st on wrong side rows

Sample Chart

1 stitch

tint indicates instruction involving more than 1 stitch

4

3

wrong side rows start this side

2

right side rows start this side

1

Rep these 3 sts

1 row

pattern repeat

stitch to balance pattern

Note: For meaning of each symbol refer to abbreviations.

Abbreviations and Symbols

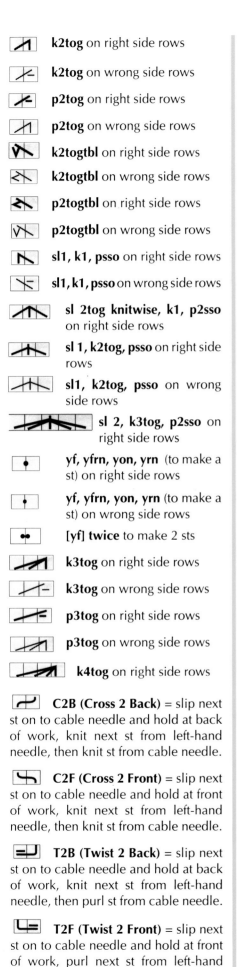

k2tog on right side rows

k2tog on wrong side rows

p2tog on right side rows

p2tog on wrong side rows

k2togtbl on right side rows

k2togtbl on wrong side rows

p2togtbl on right side rows

p2togtbl on wrong side rows

sl1, k1, psso on right side rows

sl1, k1, psso on wrong side rows

sl 2tog knitwise, k1, p2sso on right side rows

sl 1, k2tog, psso on right side rows

sl1, k2tog, psso on wrong side rows

sl 2, k3tog, p2sso on right side rows

yf, yfrn, yon, yrn (to make a st) on right side rows

yf, yfrn, yon, yrn (to make a st) on wrong side rows

[yf] twice to make 2 sts

k3tog on right side rows

k3tog on wrong side rows

p3tog on right side rows

p3tog on wrong side rows

k4tog on right side rows

C2B (Cross 2 Back) = slip next st on to cable needle and hold at back of work, knit next st from left-hand needle, then knit st from cable needle.

C2F (Cross 2 Front) = slip next st on to cable needle and hold at front of work, knit next st from left-hand needle, then knit st from cable needle.

T2B (Twist 2 Back) = slip next st on to cable needle and hold at back of work, knit next st from left-hand needle, then purl st from cable needle.

T2F (Twist 2 Front) = slip next st on to cable needle and hold at front of work, purl next st from left-hand needle, then knit st from cable needle.

T2BW(Twist 2 Back on Wrong side) = slip next st on to cable needle and hold at back (right side) of work, knit next st from left-hand needle, then purl st from cable needle.

T2FW (Twist 2 Front on Wrong side) = slip next stitch on to cable needle and hold at front (wrong side) of work, purl next st from left-hand needle, then knit st from cable needle.

C3B (Cable 3 Back) = slip next st on to cable needle and hold at back of work, knit next 2 sts from left-hand needle, then knit st from cable needle.

C3F (Cable 3 Front) = slip next 2 sts on to cable needle and hold at front of work, knit next st from left-hand needle, then knit sts from cable needle.

C3R (Cable 3 Right) = slip next 2 sts on to cable needle and hold at back of work, knit next st from left-hand needle, then knit sts from cable needle.

C3L(Cable 3 Left) = slip next st on to cable needle and hold at front of work, knit next 2 sts from left-hand needle, then knit st from cable needle.

T3B (Twist 3 Back) = slip next st on to cable needle and hold at back of work, knit next 2 sts from left-hand needle, then purl st from cable needle.

T3F (Twist 3 Front) = slip next 2 sts on to cable needle and hold at front of work, purl next st from left-hand needle, then knit sts from cable needle.

C4B (Cable 4 Back) = slip next 2 sts on to cable needle and hold at back of work, knit next 2 sts from left-hand needle, then knit sts from cable needle.

C4F (Cable 4 Front) = slip next 2 sts on to cable needle and hold at front of work, knit next 2 sts from left-hand needle, then knit sts from cable needle.

T4B (Twist 4 Back) = slip next 2 sts on to cable needle and hold at back of work, knit next 2 sts from left-hand needle, then purl sts from cable needle.

T4F (Twist 4 Front) = slip next 2 sts on to cable needle and hold at front of work, purl next 2 sts from left-hand needle, then knit sts from cable needle.

T4R (Twist 4 Right) = slip next st on to cable needle and hold at back of work, knit next 3 sts from left-hand needle, then purl st from cable needle.

T4L (Twist 4 Left) = slip next 3 sts on to cable needle and hold at front of work, purl next st from left-hand needle, then knit sts from cable needle.

T5R (Twist 5 Right) = slip next 2 sts on to cable needle and hold at back of work, knit next 3 sts from left-hand needle, then purl sts from cable needle.

T5L (Twist 5 Left) = slip next 3 sts on to cable needle and hold at front of work, purl next 2 sts from left-hand needle, then knit sts from cable needle.

T5BP (Twist 5 Back Purl) = slip next 3 sts on to cable needle and hold at back of work, knit next 2 sts from left-hand needle, then purl 1, k2 from cable needle.

C6B (Cable 6 Back) = slip next 3 sts on to cable needle and hold at back of work, knit next 3 sts from left-hand needle, then knit sts from cable needle.

C6F (Cable 6 Front) = slip next 3 sts on to cable needle and hold at front of work, knit next 3 sts from left-hand needle, then knit sts from cable needle.

C8B (Cable 8 Back) = slip next 4 sts on to cable needle and hold at back of work, knit next 4 sts from left-hand needle, then knit sts from cable needle.

C8F (Cable 8 Front) = slip next 4 sts on to cable needle and hold at front of work, knit next 4 sts from left-hand needle, then knit sts from cable needle.

C12B (Cable 12 Back) = slip next 6 sts on to cable needle and hold at back of work, knit next 6 sts from left-hand needle, then knit sts from cable needle.

C12F (Cable 12 Front) = slip next 6 sts on to cable needle and hold at front of work, knit next 6 sts from left-hand needle, then knit sts from cable needle.

Ribbed Cardigan

Measurements

To fit bust size	75/80	85/90	95/100	cm
	30/32	34/36	38/40	ins
Finished measurement	104	114	124	cm
	41½	45½	49½	ins
Length to shoulder	71	73	75	cm
	28	28¾	29½	ins
Sleeve length	45	45	46	cm
	17¾	17¾	18	ins

Shown in 85/90 cm [34/36 inch] size.

Materials

4 ply knitting yarn	500	550	625	grams
	18	20	23	ounces

Pair needles size 3¼mm (UK 10, USA 3 or 4). 3¼mm (UK 10, USA 3 or 4) circular needle 100 cm [40 ins] long. 3.25mm (UK 10, USA 3) crochet hook. 5 buttons. 4.5 metres [5 yards] velvet ribbon for appliqué.

The quantities of yarn stated are based on average requirements and are therefore approximate.

For abbreviations see pages 18 and 19.

Tension

37 sts and 36 rows = 10 cm [4 ins] square measured over rib.

Special Abbreviation

MB (Make Bobble) = work [k1, yf, k1, yf, k1] into next st, [turn and k5, turn and p5] twice, turn and k2tog, k1, k2tog, turn and p3tog (bobble completed).

Left Front

Cast on 99(109-117) sts.

1st row (right side): K1, *p1, k1; rep from * to end.

2nd row: P1, *k1, p1; rep from * to end.

Rep the last 2 rows until front measures 66(68-70) cm [26(26¾-27½) ins] or 5 cm [2 ins] less than required length to shoulder, ending with a right side row. (Work 1 row more here for Right Front).

Shape Neck

Next row: In rib, cast off 22(26-29) sts, rib to end.

Keeping rib correct, dec 1 st at neck edge on next 16 rows. 61(67-72)

sts remain. Work 2 rows straight thus ending at side edge.

Shape Shoulders

In rib, cast off 20(22-24) sts at beg of next and following alt row. Work 1 row. Cast off remaining 21(23-24) sts.

Right Front

Work as given for Left Front reversing shaping by working 1 row more where indicated.

Back

Cast on 193(211-229) sts and work in rib as given for Left Front until back measures same as left front to start of shoulder shaping ending with a wrong side row.

Shape Shoulders

In rib, cast off 20(22-24) sts at beg of next 4 rows, then 21(23-24) sts at beg of following 2 rows. Cast off remaining 71(77-85) sts.

Sleeves

Cast on 93(95-97) sts and work 2 rows in rib as given for Left Front. Bringing extra sts into rib, inc 1 st at each end of next and every following 4th(4th-2nd) row until there are 113(151-107) sts, then every following 6th(6th-4th) row until there are 149(163-177) sts. Work straight until sleeve measures

45(45-46) cm [17¾(17¾-18) ins] ending with a wrong side row. Cast off in rib.

Finishing and Edgings

Block but do not press. Join shoulder seams.

Neck Edging

With right side of work facing, pick up and knit 16(18-22) sts across cast off edge at right front neck, 17 sts up slope to shoulder, 53(57-65) sts across back neck, 17 sts down left front slope, then 16(18-22) sts across cast off edge. 119(127-143) sts.

Next row: K7, *MB, k7; rep from * to end.

Knit 1 row, then cast off purlwise.

Sleeve Cuff Edging

With right side of work facing pick up and k73 sts along cast on edge of sleeve.

Next row: K4, *MB, k7; rep from * to last 5 sts, MB, k4.

Knit 1 row, then cast off purlwise.

Lower Edging

Using circular needle and with right side of work facing, pick up and knit 74(81-89) sts along cast on edge of left front, 147(157-173) sts along back, then 74(81-89) sts along right front. 295(319-351) sts. Turning at end of every row complete as given for Neck Edging.

Fold edgings in half to inside and slip-stitch in place.

Left Front Edging

Using crochet hook and with right side of work facing, work 2 rows of firm dc along left front edge. Fasten off.

Mark positions 2 cm [¾ inch] in from left front edge for 5 buttons, the first 18 cm [7 ins] from lower edge and the last 2 cm [¾ inch] below start of neck shaping, space the remaining buttons evenly between.

Right Front Edging

Using crochet hook and with right side of work facing, work 1 row of

Ribbed Cardigan

firm dc along right front edge, then work a 2nd row of dc making 5 buttonloops to correspond with markers by working 4ch in place of 2dc. Fasten off.

Fold each sleeve in half lengthways and mark centre of cast off edge. Sew each sleeve to a side edge placing centre at shoulder seam.

Note: Armholes should measure approximately 20(22-24 cm) [8(8³/4-9¹/2) ins]. Join side and sleeve seams.

Sew on buttons.

Cut ribbon into 25cm [10 ins] lengths and slip-stitch to lower edges of sleeves and body as illustrated in photograph.

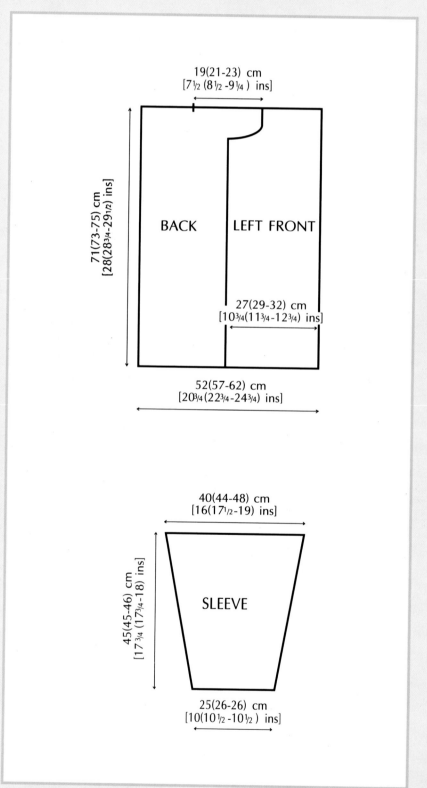

19(21-23) cm
[7¹/2 (8¹/2 -9¹/4) ins]

71(73-75) cm
[28(28³/4-29¹/2) ins]

BACK   LEFT FRONT

27(29-32) cm
[10³/4(11³/4-12³/4) ins]

52(57-62) cm
[20³/4(22³/4-24³/4) ins]

40(44-48) cm
[16(17¹/2-19) ins]

45(45-46) cm
[17³/4 (17³/4-18) ins]

SLEEVE

25(26-26) cm
[10(10¹/2-10¹/2) ins]

Ribs with Bobbles

Little Bobble Rib

Multiple of 8 sts + 3.

Special Abbreviation

⬤ **MB (Make Bobble)** = [p1, k1, p1, k1] into next st, then pass 2nd, 3rd and 4th sts separately over first st (bobble completed).

1st row (right side): K3, *p5, k3; rep from * to end.

2nd row: P3, *k5, p3; rep from * to end.

3rd row: K3, *p2, MB, p2, k3; rep from * to end.

4th row: As 2nd row.

Rep these 4 rows.

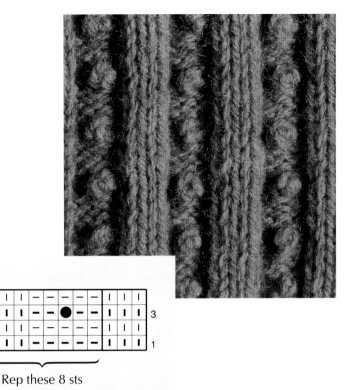

Rep these 8 sts

Large Bobble Rib

Multiple of 7 sts + 2.

Special Abbreviation

⬤ **MB (Make Bobble)** = knit into front, back and front of next st, turn and k3, turn and p3, turn and k3, turn and sl 1, k2tog, psso (bobble completed).

1st row (right side): K2, *p2, k1, p2, k2; rep from * to end.

2nd row: P2, *k2, p1, k2, p2; rep from * to end.

3rd row: K2, *p2, MB, p2, k2; rep from * to end.

4th row: As 2nd row.

Rep these 4 rows.

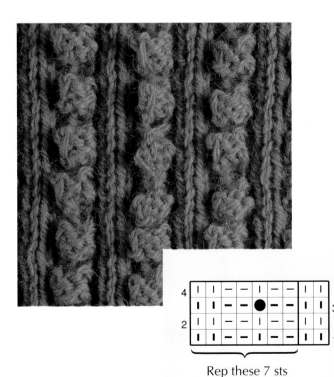

Rep these 7 sts

Lacy Ribs

Double Lace Rib

Multiple of 6 sts + 2.

1st row (right side): K2, *p1, yon, k2togtbl, p1, k2; rep from * to end.

2nd row: P2, *k1, p2; rep from * to end.

3rd row: K2, *p1, k2tog, yfrn, p1, k2; rep from * to end.

4th row: As 2nd row.

Rep these 4 rows.

Rep these 6 sts

Rib with Eyelets

Multiple of 4 sts + 1.

1st row (right side): K1, *p3, k1; rep from * to end.

2nd row: P1, *k3, p1; rep from * to end.

3rd and 4th rows: Rep 1st and 2nd rows once more.

5th row: K1, *p2tog, yrn, p1, k1; rep from * to end.

6th row: As 2nd row.

Rep these 6 rows.

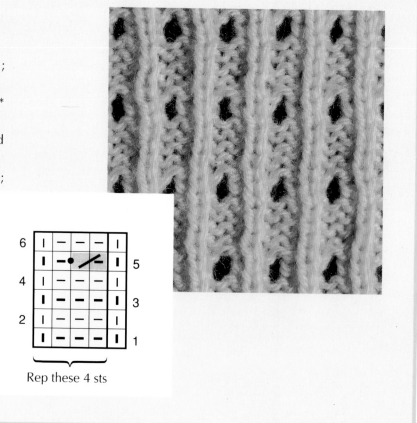

Rep these 4 sts

Diamond Rib

Multiple of 9 sts + 2.

1st row (right side): P2, *k2tog, [k1, yf] twice, k1, sl 1, k1, psso, p2; rep from * to end.

2nd and every alt row: K2, *p7, k2; rep from * to end.

3rd row: P2, *k2tog, yf, k3, yf, sl 1, k1, psso, p2; rep from * to end.

5th row: P2, *k1, yf, sl 1, k1, psso, k1, k2tog, yf, k1, p2; rep from * to end.

7th row: P2, *k2, yf, sl 1, k2tog, psso, yf, k2, p2; rep from * to end.

8th row: As 2nd row.

Rep these 8 rows.

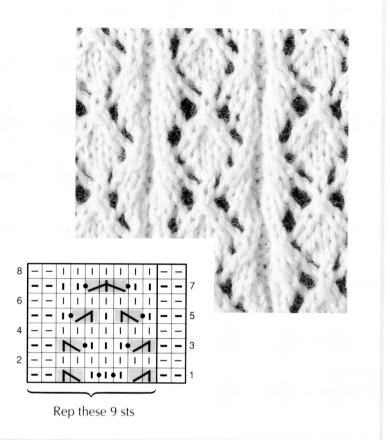

Rep these 9 sts

Large Eyelet Rib

Multiple of 6 sts + 2.

1st row (right side): *P2, k2tog, [yf] twice, sl 1, k1, psso; rep from * to last 2 sts, p2.

2nd row: K2, *p1, [k1, p1] into double yf of previous row, p1, k2; rep from * to end.

3rd row: *P2, k4; rep from * to last 2 sts, p2.

4th row: K2, *p4, k2; rep from * to end.

Rep these 4 rows.

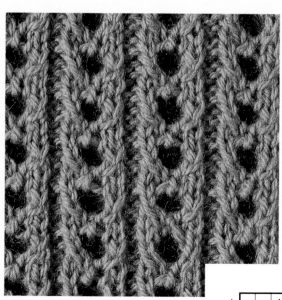

Rep these 6 sts

Cable Ribs

Mock Cable - Left

Multiple of 4 sts + 2.

1st row (right side): P2, *k2, p2; rep from * to end.

2nd row: K2, *p2, k2; rep from * to end.

3rd row: P2, *C2F, p2; rep from * to end.

4th row: As 2nd row.

Rep these 4 rows.

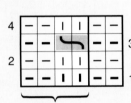

Rep these 4 sts

Mock Cable - Right

Multiple of 4 sts + 2.

1st row (right side): P2, *k2, p2; rep from * to end.

2nd row: K2, *p2, k2; rep from * to end.

3rd row: P2, *C2B, p2; rep from * to end.

4th row: As 2nd row.

Rep these 4 rows.

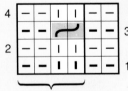

Rep these 4 sts

Tracery Rib

Multiple of 8 sts + 2.

Note: Slip all sl sts with yarn at wrong side of work.

1st row (right side): P2, *k6, p2; rep from * to end.

2nd row: K2, *p6, k2; rep from * to end.

3rd row: P2, *C3R, C3L, p2; rep from * to end.

4th row: K2, *sl 1, p4, sl 1, k2; rep from * to end.

5th row: P2, *sl 1, k1, psso, yf, C2B, yf, k2tog, p2; rep from * to end.

6th and 7th rows: Rep 4th and 5th rows once more.

8th row: As 2nd row.

9th row: P2, *C3L, C3R, p2; rep from * to end.

10th row: As 2nd row.

Rep these 10 rows.

Rep these 8 sts

Cable and Eyelet Rib

Multiple of 10 sts + 4.

1st row (right side): P1, k2tog, yfrn, *p2, k4, p2, k2tog, yfrn; rep from * to last st, p1.

2nd row: K1, p2, *k2, p4, k2, p2; rep from * to last st, k1.

3rd row: P1, yon, sl 1, k1, psso, *p2, C4F, p2, yon, sl 1, k1, psso; rep from * to last st, p1.

4th row: As 2nd row.

5th and 6th rows: As 1st and 2nd rows.

7th rows: P1, yon, sl 1, k1, psso, *p2, k4, p2, yon, sl 1, k1, psso; rep from * to last st, p1.

8th row: As 2nd row.

Rep these 8 rows.

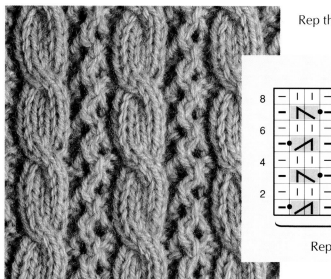

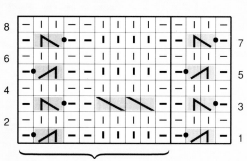

Rep these 10 sts

27

Cabled Top

Measurements

To fit bust size	80-90	95-105	cm
	32-36	38-42	ins
Finished measurement	103	123	cm
	41	49	ins
Length to shoulder (including border)	48	49	cm
	19	19¼	ins
Sleeve length (including border)	15	15	cm
	6	6	ins

Shown in 80-90 cm [32-36 inch] size.

Materials

Cotton Double Knitting yarn	500	550	grams
	18	20	ounces

Pair needles size 4mm (UK 8, USA 6).
Cable needle.

The quantities of yarn stated are based on average requirements and are therefore approximate.

For abbreviations see pages 18 and 19.

Tension

22 sts and 30 rows = 10 cm [4 ins] square measured over st st.

Special Abbreviation

Inc 1 (Increase 1 stitch) = knit into front and back of next st.

Back

Cast on 144(172) sts, work 2 rows in st st, starting knit, then 6 rows in garter st (every row knit).

Commence pattern.

1st row (right side): P14(10), k8, *p10, k8; rep from * to last 14(10) sts, p14(10).

2nd row: K14(10), p8, *k10, p8; rep from * to last 14(10) sts, k14(10).

3rd row: As 1st row.

4th row: As 2nd row.

5th row: P14(10), C8B, *p10, C8B; rep from * to last 14(10) sts, p14(10).

6th row: As 2nd row.

7th to 12th rows: Rep 1st and 2nd rows 3 times.

These 12 rows form cable pattern.

Continue in pattern until back measures 40(41) cm [15¾(16) ins], ending with a wrong side row.

Shape Shoulders

Cast off 44(52) sts at beg of next 2 rows.

Cast off remaining 56(68) sts.

Front

Work as given for Back until front is 18(22) rows shorter than back to start of shoulder shaping, thus ending with a wrong side row.

Shape Neck

Next row: Work 56(68) sts in pattern, turn and complete this side first.

Keeping pattern correct, dec 1 st at neck edge on next 12(16) rows. 44(52) sts remain.

Work 5 rows straight, thus ending at side edge.

Cast off.

With right side of work facing, rejoin yarn to next st, cast off 32(36) sts, work in pattern to end. Keeping pattern correct, dec 1 st at neck edge on next 12(16) rows. 44(52) sts remain. Work 6 rows straight, thus ending at side edge.

Cast off.

Sleeves

Cast on 96(100) sts, work 2 rows in st st, starting knit, then work 6 rows in garter st increasing 1 st at each end of first and following 2 alt rows. 102(106) sts.

Commence pattern.

1st row: Inc 1, p1(3), k8, *p10, k8; rep from * to last 2(4) sts, p0(2), Inc 1, p1.104(108) sts.

2nd row: K3(5), p8, *k10, p8; rep from * to last 3(5) sts, k3(5).

Keeping pattern correct as set, inc 1 st at each end of next row. Work 1 row straight.

Working C8B in place of each k8 on next and following 6th row, bringing extra sts into reverse st st, continue to inc 1 st at each end of next and following 2 alt rows. 112(116) sts. Work 5 rows straight. Cast off in pattern.

Collar

Cast on 11 sts and commence pattern.

1st row (right side): Cast on 2 sts, cast off 2 sts, slip st on right-hand needle back on to left-hand needle, cast on 3 sts, cast off 3 sts, slip st back on to left-hand needle, cast on 2 sts, cast off 2 sts, slip st back on to left-hand needle, k1, [k2tog, yf] twice, [k2tog] twice, yf, k2. 10 sts.

2nd and every alt row: Knit.

3rd row: K2, yf, [k2tog, yf, k2] twice. 11 sts.

5th row: K2, yf, k2tog, yf, k3, k2tog, yf, k2. 12 sts.

7th row: Cast on 2 sts, cast off 2 sts, k2 (including st on needle after cast off) yf, k2tog, yf, k4, k2tog, yf, k2. 13 sts.

9th row: K2, yf, k2tog, yf, k5, k2tog, yf, k2. 14 sts.

11th row: Cast on 2 sts, cast off 2 sts, slip st on right-hand needle back on to left-hand needle, cast on 3 sts, cast off 3 sts, slip st on right-hand needle back on to left-hand needle, cast on 2 sts, cast off 2 sts, slip st on right-hand needle back on to left-hand needle, k2, yf, k2tog, yf, k6, k2tog, yf, k2. 15 sts.

Cabled Top

13th row: K1, [k2tog, yf] twice, k2tog, k4, k2tog, yf, k2. 14 sts.

15th row: Cast on 2 sts, cast off 2 sts (1 st on right-hand needle), [k2tog, yf] twice, k2tog, k3, k2tog, yf, k2. 13 sts.

17th row: K1, [k2tog, yf] twice, k2tog, k2, k2tog, yf, k2. 12 sts.

19th row: K1, [k2tog, yf] twice, k2tog, k1, k2tog, yf, k2. 11 sts.

20th row: Knit.

These 20 rows form the pattern. Rep these 20 rows 6(7) times more then 1st and 2nd rows once more. Cast off.

Lower Border

Work as given for Collar until the 20 rows have been worked 12(13) times in all. Cast off.

Sleeve Borders

Work as given for Collar until the 20 rows have been worked 5 times in all. Cast off.

To Finish

Block but do not press.

Join shoulder seams. Fold each sleeve in half lengthways and mark

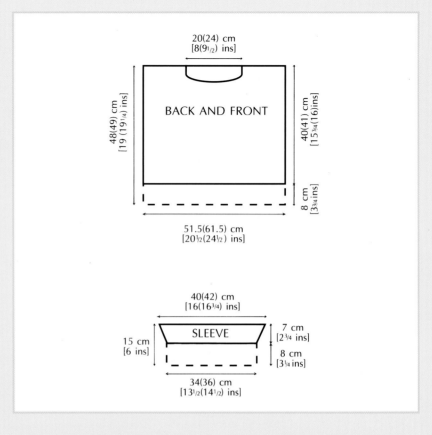

20(24) cm [8(9½) ins]

48(49) cm [19 (19¼) ins]

BACK AND FRONT

40(41) cm [15¾(16)ins]

8 cm [3¾ ins]

51.5(61.5) cm [20½(24½) ins]

40(42) cm [16(16¾) ins]

SLEEVE

15 cm [6 ins]

7 cm [2¾ ins]

8 cm [3¼ ins]

34(36) cm [13½(14½) ins]

centre of cast off edge. Sew each sleeve to a side edge placing centre at shoulder seam. Join side and sleeve seams.

Starting at centre back, sew collar evenly around neck edge. Join lower border into a ring and, placing seam at one side seam, sew evenly in place along back and front cast on edge. Join sleeve border into a ring and, placing seam at sleeve seam, sew evenly in place along cast on edge of sleeves.

Wavy Border

Worked lengthways starting with 13 sts.

1st and every alt row (wrong side): K2, purl to last 2 sts, k2.

2nd row: Sl 1, k3, yf, k5, yf, k2tog, yf, k2. (15 sts)

4th row: Sl 1, k4, sl 1, k2tog, psso, k2, [yf, k2tog] twice, k1. (13 sts)

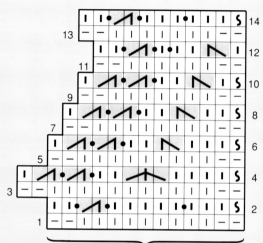

Start with 13 sts

6th row: Sl 1, k3, sl 1, k1, psso, k2, [yf, k2tog] twice, k1. (12 sts)

8th row: Sl 1, k2, sl 1, k1, psso, k2, [yf, k2tog] twice, k1. (11 sts)

10th row: Sl 1, k1, sl 1, k1, psso, k2, [yf, k2tog] twice, k1. (10 sts)

12th row: K1, sl 1, k1, psso, k2, yf, k1, yf, k2tog, yf, k2. (11 sts)

14th row: Sl 1, [k3, yf] twice, k2tog, yf, k2. (13 sts)

Rep these 14 rows.

Butterfly Edging

Worked lengthways starting with 8 sts.

Note: Count [yf] twice as 2 sts.

1st row (right side): Sl 1, k2, yf, k2tog, [yf] twice, k2tog, k1. (9 sts)

2nd row: K3, p1, k2, yf, k2tog, k1.

3rd row: Sl 1, k2, yf, k2tog, k1, [yf] twice, k2tog, k1. (10 sts)

4th row: K3, p1, k3, yf, k2tog, k1.

5th row: Sl 1, k2, yf, k2tog, k2 [yf] twice, k2tog, k1. (11 sts)

6th row: K3, p1, k4, yf, k2tog, k1.

7th row: Sl 1, k2, yf, k2tog, k6.

8th row: Cast off 3 sts (1 st on right-hand needle), k4, yf, k2tog, k1. (8 sts)

Rep these 8 rows.

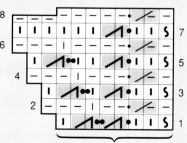

Start with 8 sts

31

Lacy Edgings

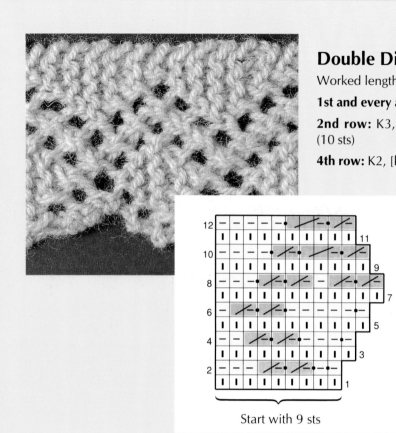

Double Diamond Edging

Worked lengthways starting with 9 sts.

1st and every alt row (right side): Knit.

2nd row: K3, k2tog, yf, k2tog, [yf, k1] twice. (10 sts)

4th row: K2, [k2tog, yf] twice, k3, yf, k1. (11 sts)

6th row: K1, [k2tog, yf] twice, k5, yf, k1. (12 sts)

8th row: K3, [yf, k2tog] twice, k1, k2tog, yf, k2tog. (11 sts)

10th row: K4, yf, k2tog, yf, k3tog, yf, k2tog. (10 sts)

12th row: K5, yf, k3tog, yf, k2tog. (9 sts)

Rep these 12 rows.

Start with 9 sts

Lacy Arrow Edging

Worked lengthways. Cast on 21 sts.

1st row (right side): K3, yf, k2tog, p2, yon, sl 1, k1, psso, k3, k2tog, yfrn, p2, k1, yf, k2tog, k2.

2nd and every alt row: K3, yf, k2togtbl, k2, p7, k3, yf, k2togtbl, k2.

3rd row: K3, yf, k2tog, p2, k2, yf, sl 1, k1, psso, k1, k2tog, yf, k1, p2, k1, yf, k2tog, k2.

5th row: K3, yf, k2tog, p2, k2, yf, sl 1, k2tog, psso, yf, k2, p2, k1, yf, k2tog, k2.

6th row: As 2nd row.

Rep these 6 rows.

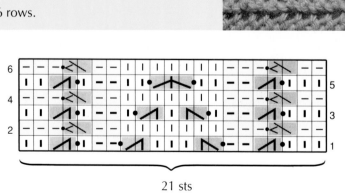

21 sts

Laburnum Edging

Worked lengthways starting with 13 sts.

Note: Count [yf] twice as 2 sts.

Special Abbreviation

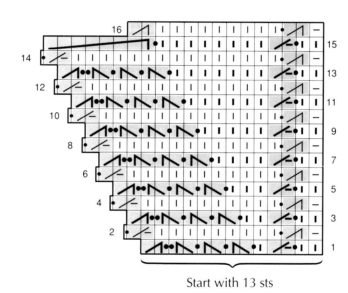 **Pass 7 over =** slip last st worked back on to left-hand needle and with point of right-hand needle pass next 7 sts over this st and off, slip st back on to right-hand needle.

Start with 13 sts

1st row (right side): K2, yfrn, p2tog, k1, [yf, sl 1, k1, psso] 3 times, [yf] twice, k2tog. (14 sts)

2nd row: Yf (to make a stitch), k2tog, p9, yrn, p2tog, k1.

3rd row: K2, yfrn, p2tog, k2, [yf, sl 1, k1, psso] 3 times, [yf] twice, k2tog. (15 sts)

4th row: Yf, k2tog, p10, yrn, p2tog, k1.

5th row: K2, yfrn, p2tog, k3, [yf, sl 1, k1, psso] 3 times, [yf] twice, k2tog. (16 sts)

6th row: Yf, k2tog, p11, yrn, p2tog, k1.

7th row: K2, yfrn, p2tog, k4, [yf, sl 1, k1, psso] 3 times, [yf] twice, k2tog. (17 sts)

8th row: Yf, k2tog, p12, yrn, p2tog, k1.

9th row: K2, yfrn, p2tog, k5, [yf, sl 1, k1, psso] 3 times, [yf] twice, k2tog. (18 sts) `

10th row: Yf, k2tog, p13, yrn, p2tog, k1.

11th row: K2, yfrn, p2tog, k6, [yf, sl 1, k1, psso] 3 times, [yf] twice, k2tog. (19 sts)

12th row: Yf, k2tog, p14, yrn, p2tog, k1.

13th row: K2, yfrn, p2tog, k7, [yf, sl 1, k1, psso] 3 times, [yf] twice, k2tog. (20 sts)

14th row: Yf, k2tog, p15, yrn, p2tog, k1.

15th row: K2, yfrn, p2tog, k8, yf, k1, Pass 7 over. (14 sts)

16th row: P2tog, p9, yrn, p2tog, k1. (13 sts)

Rep these 16 rows.

Lacy Edgings

2nd row: K3, [p1, k2] twice, yf, k2tog, k1.

3rd row: Sl 1, k2, yf, k2tog, k2, *[yf] twice, k2tog; rep from * once more, k1. (14 sts)

4th row: K3, p1, k2, p1, k4, yf, k2tog, k1.

5th row: Sl 1, k2, yf, k2tog, k4, *[yf] twice, k2tog; rep from * once more, k1. (16 sts)

6th row: K3, p1, k2, p1, k6, yf, k2tog, k1.

7th row: Sl 1, k2, yf, k2tog, k11.

8th row: Cast off 6 sts, k6 (not including st already on needle after casting off), yf, k2tog, k1. (10 sts)

Rep these 8 rows.

Willow Edging

Worked lengthways starting with 10 sts.

Note: Count [yf] twice as 2 sts.

1st row (right side): Sl 1, k2, yf, k2tog, *[yf] twice, k2tog; rep from * once more, k1. (12 sts)

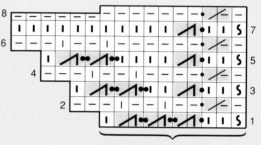

Start with 10 sts

Diamond Edging

Worked lengthways starting with 12 sts.

1st and every alt row (right side): K1, yfrn, p2tog, knit to end.

2nd row: K2, yf, k3, yf, sl 1, k1, psso, k2, yfrn, p2tog, k1. (13 sts)

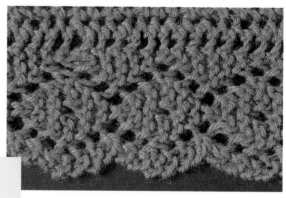

4th row: K2, yf, k5, yf, sl 1, k1, psso, k1, yfrn, p2tog, k1. (14 sts)

6th row: K2, yf, k3, yf, sl 1, k1, psso, k2, yf, sl 1, k1, psso, yfrn, p2tog, k1. (15 sts)

8th row: K1, k2tog, yf, sl 1, k1, psso, k3, k2tog, yf, k2, yfrn, p2tog, k1.

10th row: K1, k2tog, yf, sl 1, k1, psso, k1, k2tog, yf, k3, yfrn, p2tog, k1. (14 sts)

12th row: K1, k2tog, yf, sl 1, k2tog, psso, yf, k4, yfrn, p2tog, k1.

Rep these 12 rows.

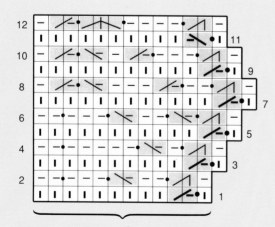

Start with 12 sts

6th row: K4, p2, k1, p4, k2, yfrn, p2tog, yrn, p2tog, k1.

7th row: K3, yfrn, p2tog, yrn, p2tog, yon, KB1, k1, KB1, yf, sl 1, k2tog, psso, yf, k5. (19 sts).

8th row: K5, p7, k2, yfrn, p2tog, yrn, p2tog, k1.

9th row: K3, yfrn, p2tog, yrn, p2tog, yon, KB1, k3, KB1, yf, k7. (21 sts).

Fancy Leaf Edging

Worked lengthways starting with 17 sts.

1st row (right side): K3, yfrn, p2tog, yrn, p2tog, yon, KB1, k2tog, p1, yb, sl 1, k1, psso, KB1, yf, k3.

2nd row: K3, p3, k1, p3, k2, yfrn, p2tog, yrn, p2tog, k1.

3rd and 4th rows: Rep 1st and 2nd rows once more.

5th row: K3, yfrn, p2tog, yrn, p2tog, yon, KB1, yf, k2tog, p1, yb, sl 1, k1, psso, yf, k4. (18 sts).

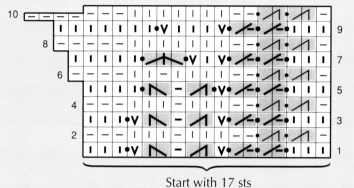

Start with 17 sts

10th row: Cast off 4 sts (1 st remains on right-hand needle), k2, p7, k2, yfrn, p2tog, yrn, p2tog, k1. (17 sts).

Rep these 10 rows.

Double Beaded Edge

Worked lengthways, starting with 8 sts.

1st row (right side): Sl 1, k1, *yfrn, p2tog, [k1, p1, k1] into next st; rep from * once more. (12 sts).

2nd row: [K3, yfrn, p2tog] twice, k2.

3rd row: Sl 1, k1, [yfrn, p2tog, k3] twice.

4th row: Cast off 2 sts knitwise (1 st remains on right-hand needle), yfrn, p2tog, cast off next 2 sts knitwise (4 sts on right-hand needle), yfrn, p2tog, k2. (8 sts).

Rep these 4 rows.

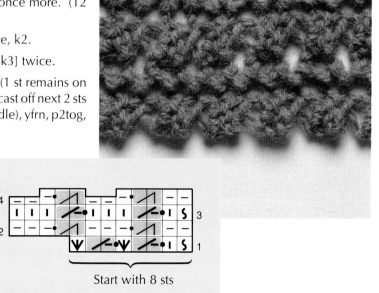

Start with 8 sts

Edgings

Scallop Edging

Cast on a multiple of 13 sts + 2. (The number of sts varies within the pattern).

1st row (right side): K3, *sl 1, k1, psso, sl 2, k3tog, p2sso, k2tog, k4; rep from * to last 12 sts, sl 1, k1, psso, sl 2, k3tog, p2sso, k2tog, k3.

2nd row: P4, *yrn, p1, yrn, p6; rep from * to last 5 sts, yrn, p1, yrn, p4.

3rd row: K1, yf, *k2, sl 1, k1, psso, k1, k2tog, k2, yf; rep from * to last st, k1.

4th row: P2, *yrn, p2, yrn, p3, yrn, p2, yrn, p1; rep from * to last st, p1.

5th row: K2, yf, k1, *yf, sl 1, k1, psso, k1, sl 1, k2tog, psso, k1, k2tog, [yf, k1] 3 times; rep from * to last 12 sts, yf, sl 1, k1, psso, k1, sl 1, k2tog, psso, k1, k2tog, yf, k1, yf, k2.

6th row: Purl.

7th row: K5, *yf, sl 2, k3tog, p2sso, yf, k7; rep from * to last 10 sts, yf, sl 2, k3tog, p2sso, yf, k5.

8th to 11th rows: Knit.

These 11 rows complete the edging.

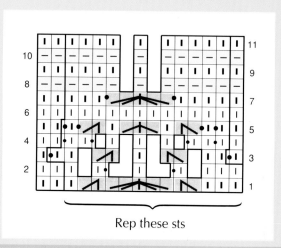

Rep these sts

Bell Edging

Cast on a multiple of 12 sts + 3.

Note: 2 sts are decreased for every repeat on 3rd and following alt rows.

1st row (right side): P3, *k9, p3; rep from * to end.

2nd row: K3, *p9, k3; rep from * to end.

3rd row: P3, *yb, sl 1, k1, psso, k5, k2tog, p3; rep from * to end.

4th row: K3, *p7, k3; rep from * to end.

5th row: P3, *yb, sl 1, k1, psso, k3, k2tog, p3; rep from * to end.

6th row: K3, *p5, k3; rep from * to end.

7th row: P3, *yb, sl 1, k1, psso, k1, k2tog, p3; rep from * to end.

8th row: K3, *p3, k3; rep from * to end.

9th row: P3, *yb, sl 1, k2tog, psso, p3; rep from * to end.

10th row: K3, *p1, k3; rep from * to end.

11th row: P3, *k1, p3; rep from * to end.

12th row: As 10th row.

These 12 rows complete the edging.

Rep these sts

Lace Bells

Cast on a multiple of 14 sts + 3 using thumb method.

Note: 2 sts are decreased for every repeat on 5th and following alt rows.

1st row (right side): Knit.

2nd row: Knit.

3rd row: P3, *k11, p3; rep from * to end.

4th row: K3, *p11, k3; rep from * to end.

5th row: P3, *yb, sl 1, k1, psso, k2, yf, sl 1, k2tog, psso, yf, k2, k2tog, p3; rep from * to end.

6th row: K3, *p9, k3; rep from * to end.

7th row: P3, *yb, sl 1, k1, psso, k1, yf, sl 1, k2tog, psso, yf, k1, k2tog, p3; rep from * to end.

8th row: K3, *p7, k3; rep from * to end.

9th row: P3, *yb, sl 1, k1, psso, yf, sl 1, k2tog, psso, yf, k2tog, p3; rep from * to end.

10th row: K3, *p5, k3; rep from * to end.

11th row: P3, *yb, sl 1, k1, psso, k1, k2tog, p3; rep from * to end.

12th row: K3, *p3, k3; rep from * to end.

13th row: P3, *yb, sl 1, k2tog, psso, p3; rep from * to end.

14th row: K3, *p1, k3; rep from * to end.

15th row: P3, *k1, p3; rep from * to end.

16th row: As 14th row.

These 16 rows complete the edging.

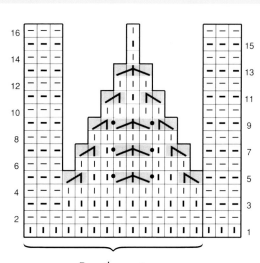

Rep these sts

Birds Eye Edging

Worked lengthways, starting with 7 sts.

Note: Count [yf] twice as 2 sts.

1st row (right side): K1, k2tog, [yf] twice, k2tog, [yf] twice, k2. (9 sts)

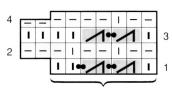

Start with 7 sts

2nd row: K3, [p1, k2] twice.

3rd row: K1, k2tog, [yf] twice, k2tog, k4.

4th row: Cast off 2 sts, k3 (not including st already on needle after casting off), p1, k2. (7sts)

Rep these 4 rows.

Long Lacy Sweater

Measurements

To fit bust size	75/80	85/90	95/100	105/110	cm
	30/32	34/36	38/40	42/44	ins
Finished measurement	82	92	102	112	cm
	33	37	41	45	ins
Length to shoulder	59	62	64	67	cm
(approximately)	23¹/2	24³/4	25¹/2	26³/4	ins
Sleeve length	43	45	45	45	cm
(approximately)	17¹/4	18	18	18	ins

Shown in 85/90 cm [34/36 inch] size.

Materials

4 ply knitting yarn	350	400	450	500	grams
	13	15	16	18	ounces

Pair needles size 3¹/4mm (UK 10, USA 3 or 4).

2.50mm (UK 12, USA C) crochet hook.

The quantites of yarn stated are based on average requirements and are therefore approximate.

For abbreviations see pages 18 and 19.

Tension

30 sts and 42 rows = 10 cm [4 ins] square measured over pattern.

Note: Where a number of sts is given, this refers to the basic number and includes those lost in the pattern.

Back

Cast on 123(138-153-168) sts and commence pattern.

1st row (right side): K2, yf, k1, sl 1, k1, psso, p1, k2tog, k1, yrn, p1, sl 1, k1, psso, p1, k2tog, *[yf, k1] 3 times, sl 1, k1, psso, p1, k2tog, k1, yrn, p1, sl 1, k1, psso, p1, k2tog; rep from * to last 3 sts, [yf, k1] twice, k1.

2nd row: P6, k1, p1, k1, p3, k1, *p8, k1, p1, k1, p3, k1; rep from * to last 5 sts, p5.

3rd row: K2, yf, k1, sl 1, k1, psso, p1, k2tog, k1, p1, sl 1, k2tog, psso, yf, k3, *[yf, k1] twice, sl 1, k1, psso, p1, k2tog, k1, p1, sl 1, k2tog, psso, yf, k3; rep from * to last 2 sts, yf, k2.

4th row: P8, k1, p2, k1, *p10, k1, p2, k1; rep from * to last 5 sts, p5.

5th row: K1, *[k1, yf] twice, sl 1, k1, psso, p1, [k2tog] twice, yf, k5, yf; rep from * to last 2 sts, k2.

6th row: P9, k1, p1, k1, *p12, k1, p1, k1; rep from * to last 6 sts, p6.

7th row: K2, yf, k3, yf, sl 1, k2tog, psso, p1, yon, k1, sl 1, k1, psso, p1, k2tog, *[k1, yf] twice, k3, yf, sl 1, k2tog, psso, p1, yon, k1, sl 1, k1, psso, p1, k2tog; rep from * to last 3 sts, k1, yf, k2.

8th row: P5, k1, p3, k1, *p10, k1, p3, k1; rep from * to last 8 sts, p8.

9th row: K2, yf, k5, yf, sl 1, k1, psso, k1, sl 1, k1, psso, p1, k2tog, *[k1, yf] twice, k5, yf, sl 1, k1, psso, k1, sl 1, k1, psso, p1, k2tog; rep from * to last 3 sts, k1 yf, k2.

10th row: P5, k1, p2, k1, *p11, k1, p2, k1; rep from * to last 9 sts, p9.

These 10 rows form the pattern. Continue in pattern until back measures approximately 59(62-64-67) cm [23¹/2(24³/4-25¹/2-26³/4) ins] or required length to shoulder, ending with a 10th row of pattern. Cast off.

Front

Work as given for Back until front is 30 rows shorter than back, thus ending with a 10th row of pattern.

Shape Neck

Next row (right side): Work 41(49-56-64) sts in pattern, turn and complete this side first.

★ Keeping pattern correct, dec 1 st at neck edge on next 5 rows, then on following 4 alt rows. 32(40-47-55) sts remain. Work 16 rows straight, thus ending with a 10th row of pattern. Cast off.

With right side facing, rejoin yarn to remaining 82(89-97-104) sts, cast off 41(40-41-40) sts, work in pattern to end.

Complete to match first side from ★ to end.

Sleeves

Cast on 63(63-78-78) sts and work in pattern as given for Back until sleeve measures approximately 21 cm [8¹/2 ins], ending with a 10th row of pattern.

Keeping pattern correct and bringing extra sts into st st, inc 1 st at each end of next and every following 4th(3rd-4th-3rd) row 7(29-11-30) times in all. 77(121-100-138) sts.

1st (3rd) sizes only: Inc 1 st at each end of every following 3rd row 18(16) times. 113(132) sts.

All sizes: Work 11(15-11-12) rows straight, thus ending with a 10th row of pattern. Cast off.

To Finish

Block or press according to instructions on ball band.

Join shoulder seams.

Neckband

With right side facing and crochet hook, work 1 round of dc evenly all round neck edge, join with a sl st into first dc.

Next round: *3ch, sl st into 3rd ch from hook, miss next dc, 1 dc into next dc; rep from * to end. Fasten off.

Fold each sleeve in half lengthways and mark centre of cast off edge. Sew each sleeve to a side edge placing centre at shoulder seam. Join side and sleeve seams.

Long Lacy Sweater

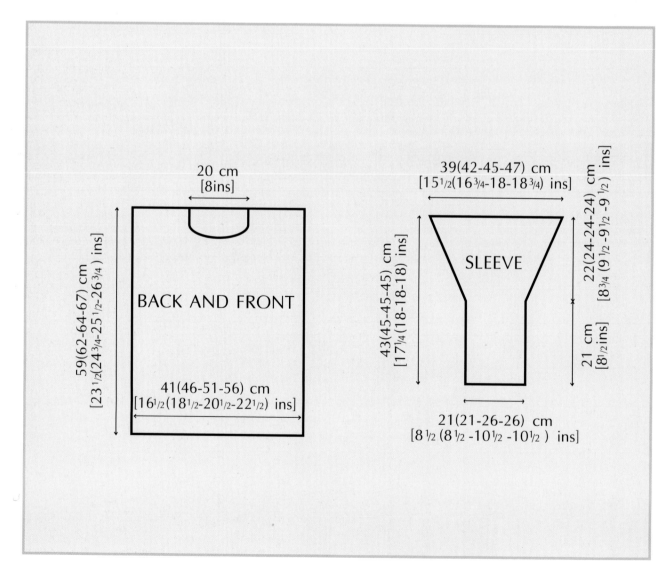

20 cm
[8ins]

39(42-45-47) cm
[15½(16¾-18-18¾) ins]

59(62-64-67) cm
[23½(24¾-25½-26¾) ins]

22(24-24-24) cm
[8¾ (9½ -9½ -9½) ins]

43(45-45-45) cm
[17¼ (18-18-18) ins]

BACK AND FRONT

SLEEVE

21 cm
[8½ins]

41(46-51-56) cm
[16½(18½-20½-22½) ins]

21(21-26-26) cm
[8½ (8½ -10½ -10½) ins]

Large All-over Lace Patterns

Oriel Lace

Multiple of 12 sts + 1.

1st row (right side): P1, *yb, sl 1, k1, psso, k3, yfrn, p1, yon, k3, k2tog, p1; rep from * to end.

2nd row: K1, *p5, k1; rep from * to end.

3rd to 6th rows: Rep 1st and 2nd rows twice more.

7th row: P1, *yon, k3, k2tog, p1, yb, sl 1, k1, psso, k3, yfrn, p1; rep from * to end.

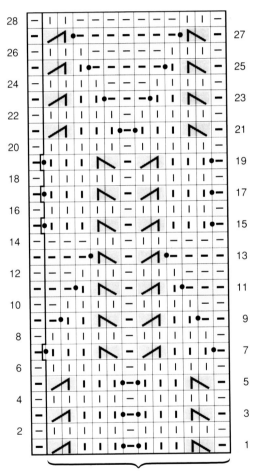

Rep these 12 sts

11th row: P3, yon, k1, k2tog, p1, yb, sl 1, k1, psso, k1, *yfrn, p5, yon, k1, k2tog, p1, yb, sl 1, k1, psso, k1; rep from * to last 3 sts, yfrn, p3.

12th row: K3, p3, k1, p3, *k5, p3, k1, p3; rep from * to last 3 sts, k3.

13th row: P4, yon, k2tog, p1, yb, sl 1, k1, psso, *yfrn, p7, yon, k2tog, p1, yb, sl 1, k1, psso; rep from * to last 4 sts, yfrn, p4.

14th row: K4, p2, k1, p2, *k7, p2, k1, p2; rep from * to last 4 sts, k4.

15th row: As 7th row.

16th row: As 2nd row.

17th to 20th rows: Rep the last 2 rows twice more.

21st row: P1, *yb, sl 1, k1, psso, k3, yfrn, p1, yon, k3, k2tog, p1; rep from * to end.

22nd row: As 2nd row.

23rd row: P1, *yb, sl 1, k1, psso, k2, yfrn, p3, yon, k2, k2tog, p1; rep from * to end.

24th row: K1, *p4, k3, p4, k1; rep from * to end.

25th row: P1, *yb, sl 1, k1, psso, k1, yfrn, p5, yon, k1, k2tog, p1; rep from * to end.

26th row: K1, *p3, k5, p3, k1; rep from * to end.

27th row: P1, *yb, sl 1, k1, psso, yfrn, p7, yon, k2tog, p1; rep from * to end.

28th row: K1, *p2, k7, p2, k1; rep from * to end.

Rep these 28 rows.

8th row: As 2nd row.

9th row: P2, yon, k2, k2tog, p1, yb, sl 1, k1, psso, k2, *yfrn, p3, yon, k2, k2tog, p1, yb, sl 1, k1, psso, k2; rep from * to last 2 sts, yfrn, p2.

10th row: K2, p4, k1, p4, *k3, p4, k1, p4; rep from * to last 2 sts, k2.

Large All-over Lace Patterns

Frost Flower Pattern

Multiple of 34 sts + 2.

1st row (right side): K4, *k2tog, k4, yfrn, p2, [k2, yf, sl 1, k1, psso] 3 times, p2, yon, k4, sl 1, k1, psso, k6; rep from * but ending last rep with k4 instead of k6.

2nd row: P3, *p2togtbl, p4, yrn, p1, k2, [p2, yrn, p2tog] 3 times, k2, p1, yrn, p4, p2tog, p4; rep from * but ending last rep with p3 instead of p4.

3rd row: K2, *k2tog, k4, yf, k2, p2, [k2, yf, sl 1, k1, psso] 3 times, p2, k2, yf, k4, sl 1, k1, psso, k2; rep from * to end.

4th row: P1, *p2togtbl, p4, yrn, p3, k2, [p2, yrn, p2tog] 3 times, k2, p3, yrn, p4, p2tog; rep from * to last st, p1.

5th to 12th rows: Rep 1st to 4th rows twice more.

13th row: K1, *yf, sl 1, k1, psso, k2, yf, sl 1, k1, psso, p2, yon, k4, sl 1, k1, psso, k6, k2tog, k4, yfrn, p2, k2, yf, sl 1, k1, psso, k2; rep from * to last st, k1.

14th row: P1, *yrn, p2tog, p2, yrn, p2tog, k2, p1, yrn, p4, p2tog, p4, p2togtbl, p4, yrn, p1, k2, p2, yrn, p2tog, p2; rep from * to last st, p1.

15th row: K1, *yf, sl 1, k1, psso, k2, yf, sl 1, k1, psso, p2, k2, yf, k4, sl 1, k1, psso, k2, k2tog, k4, yf, k2, p2, k2, yf, sl 1, k1, psso, k2; rep from * to last st, k1.

16th row: P1, *yrn, p2tog, p2, yrn, p2tog, k2, p3, yrn, p4, p2tog, p2togtbl, p4, yrn, p3, k2, p2, yrn, p2tog, p2; rep from * to last st, p1.

17th to 24th rows: Rep 13th to 16th rows twice more.

Rep these 24 rows.

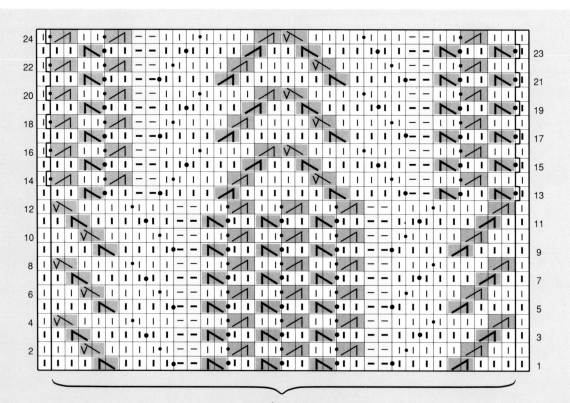

Rep these 34 sts

Entwined Leaves

Cast on a multiple of 22 sts + 21.

Note: Only count sts after 1st, 2nd, 19th and 20th rows.

1st row (right side): P2, C2B, p2, k2, sl 1, k1, psso, yf, k1, yf, k2tog, k2, p2, C2B, p2, *KB1, p2, C2B, p2, k2, sl 1, k1, psso, yf, k1, yf, k2tog, k2, p2, C2B, p2; rep from * to end.

2nd row: K2, p2, k2, p9, k2, p2, k2, *p1, k2, p2, k2, p9, k2, p2, k2; rep from * to end.

3rd row: P2, C2B, p2, yb, sl 1, k1, psso, k5, k2tog, p2, C2B, p2, *[k1, p1, k1] into next st, p2, C2B, p2, yb, sl 1, k1, psso, k5, k2tog, p2, C2B, p2; rep from * to end.

4th row: K2, p2, k2, p7, k2, p2, k2, *p3, k2, p2, k2, p7, k2, p2, k2; rep from * to end.

5th row: P2, C2B, p2, yb, sl 1, k1, psso, k3, k2tog, p2, C2B, p2, *k1, [yf, k1] twice, p2, C2B, p2, yb, sl 1, k1, psso, k3, k2tog, p2, C2B, p2; rep from * to end.

6th row: K2, p2, k2, *p5, k2, p2, k2; rep from * to end.

7th row: P2, C2B, p2, yb, sl 1, k1, psso, k1, k2tog, p2, C2B, p2, *k2, yf, k1, yf, k2, p2, C2B, p2, yb, sl 1, k1, psso, k1, k2tog, p2, C2B,

p2; rep from * to end.

8th row: K2, p2, k2, p3, k2, p2, k2, *p7, k2, p2, k2, p3, k2, p2, k2; rep from * to end.

9th row: P2, C2B, p2, yb, sl 1, k2tog, psso, p2, C2B, p2, *k3, yf, k1, yf, k3, p2, C2B, p2, yb, sl 1, k2tog, psso, p2, C2B, p2; rep from * to end.

10th row: K2, p2, k2, p1, k2, p2, k2, *p9, k2, p2, k2, p1, k2, p2, k2; rep from * to end.

11th row: P2, C2B, p2, KB1, p2, C2B, p2, *k2, sl 1, k1, psso, yf, k1, yf, k2tog, k2, p2, C2B, p2, KB1, p2, C2B, p2; rep from * to end.

12th row: As 10th row.

13th row: P2, C2B, p2, [k1, p1, k1] into next st, p2, C2B, p2, *yb, sl 1, k1, psso, k5, k2tog, p2, C2B, p2, [k1, p1, k1] into next st, p2, C2B, p2; rep from * to end.

14th row: As 8th row.

15th row: P2, C2B, p2, k1, [yf, k1] twice, p2, C2B, p2, *yb, sl 1, k1, psso, k3, k2tog, p2, C2B, p2, k1, [yf, k1] twice, p2, C2B, p2; rep from * to end.

16th row: As 6th row.

17th row: P2, C2B, p2, k2, yf, k1, yf, k2, p2, C2B, p2, *yb, sl 1, k1, psso, k1, k2tog, p2, C2B, p2, k2,

yf, k1, yf, k2, p2, C2B, p2; rep from * to end.

18th row: As 4th row.

19th row: P2, C2B, p2, k3, yf, k1, yf, k3, p2, C2B, p2, *yb, sl 1, k2tog, psso, p2, C2B, p2, k3, yf, k1, yf, k3, p2, C2B, p2; rep from * to end.

20th row: As 2nd row.

Rep these 20 rows.

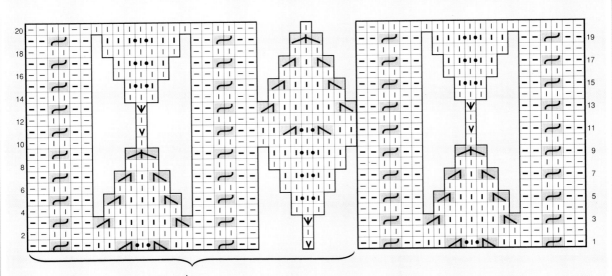

Rep these sts

Large All-over Lace Patterns

Cogwheel Eyelets

Multiple of 8 sts + 9.

1st row (right side): K2, k2tog, yf, k1, yf, sl 1, k1, psso, *k3, k2tog, yf, k1, yf, sl 1, k1, psso; rep from * to last 2 sts, k2.

2nd and every alt row: Purl.

3rd row: K1, *k2tog, yf, k3, yf, sl 1, k1, psso, k1; rep from * to end.

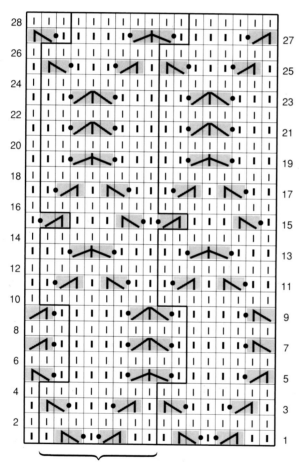

Rep these 8 sts

5th row: K2tog, yf, k5, *yf, sl 1, k2tog, psso, yf, k5; rep from * to last 2 sts, yf, sl 1, k1, psso.

7th row: Sl 1, k1, psso, yf, k5, *yf, sl 2tog knitwise, k1, p2sso, yf, k5; rep from * to last 2 sts, yf, k2tog.

9th row: As 7th row.

11th row: K2, yf, sl 1, k1, psso, k1, k2tog, yf, *k3, yf, sl 1, k1, psso, k1, k2tog, yf; rep from * to last 2 sts, k2.

13th row: K3, yf, sl 1, k2tog, psso, yf, *k5, yf, sl 1, k2tog, psso, yf; rep from * to last 3 sts, k3.

15th row: K1, *yf, sl 1, k1, psso, k3, k2tog, yf, k1; rep from * to end.

17th row: As 11th row.

19th row: As 13th row.

21st row: K3, yf, sl 2tog knitwise, k1, p2sso, yf, *k5, yf, sl 2tog knitwise, k1, p2sso, yf; rep from * to last 3 sts, k3.

23rd row: As 21st row.

25th row: As 3rd row.

27th row: As 5th row.

28th row: Purl.

Rep these 28 rows.

Large All-over Lace Patterns

Triangles and Lace

Multiple of 12 sts + 13.

1st row (right side): K1, *yf, sl 1, k1, psso, p7, k2tog, yf, k1; rep from * to end.

2nd row: P3, k7, *p5, k7; rep from * to last 3 sts, p3.

3rd row: K1, *yf, k1, sl 1, k1, psso, p5, k2tog, k1, yf, k1; rep from * to end.

4th row: P4, k5, *p7, k5; rep from * to last 4 sts, p4.

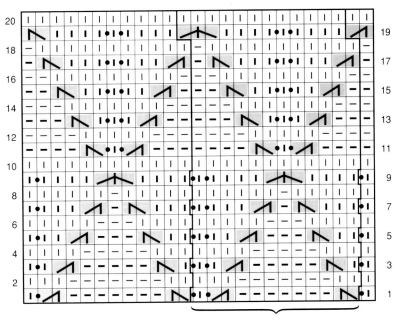

Rep these 12 sts

5th row: K1, *yf, k2, sl 1, k1, psso, p3, k2tog, k2, yf, k1; rep from * to end.

6th row: P5, k3, *p9, k3; rep from * to last 5 sts, p5.

7th row: K1, *yf, k3, sl 1, k1, psso, p1, k2tog, k3, yf, k1; rep from * to end.

8th row: P6, k1, *p11, k1; rep from * to last 6 sts, p6.

9th row: K1, *yf, k4, sl 1, k2tog, psso, k4, yf, k1; rep from * to end.

10th row: Purl.

11th row: P4, k2tog, yf, k1, yf, sl 1, k1, psso, *p7, k2tog, yf, k1, yf, sl 1, k1, psso; rep from * to last 4 sts, p4.

12th row: K4, p5, *k7, p5; rep from * to last 4 sts, k4.

13th row: P3, k2tog, k1, [yf, k1] twice, sl 1, k1, psso, *p5, k2tog, k1 [yf, k1] twice, sl 1, k1, psso; rep from * to last 3 sts, p3.

14th row: K3, p7, *k5, p7; rep from * to last 3 sts, k3.

15th row: P2, k2tog, k2, yf, k1, yf, k2, sl 1, k1, psso, *p3, k2tog, k2, yf, k1, yf, k2, sl 1, k1, psso; rep from * to last 2 sts, p2.

16th row: K2, p9, *k3, p9; rep from * to last 2 sts, k2.

17th row: P1, * k2tog, k3, yf, k1, yf, k3, sl 1, k1, psso, p1; rep from * to end.

18th row: K1, *p11, k1; rep from * to end.

19th row: K2tog, k4, yf, k1, yf, k4, *sl 1, k2tog, psso, k4, yf, k1, yf, k4; rep from * to last 2 sts, sl 1, k1, psso.

20th row: Purl.

Rep these 20 rows.

Large All-over Lace Patterns

Little and Large Diamonds

Multiple of 12 sts + 13.

1st row (right side): K1, *yf, sl 1, k1, psso, k7, k2tog, yf, k1; rep from * to end.

2nd and every alt row: Purl.

3rd row: K2, yf, sl 1, k1, psso, k5, *k2tog, yf, k3, yf, sl 1, k1, psso, k5; rep from * to last 4 sts, k2tog, yf, k2.

5th row: K3, yf, sl 1, k1, psso, k3, *k2tog, yf, k5, yf, sl 1, k1, psso, k3; rep from * to last 5 sts, k2tog, yf, k3.

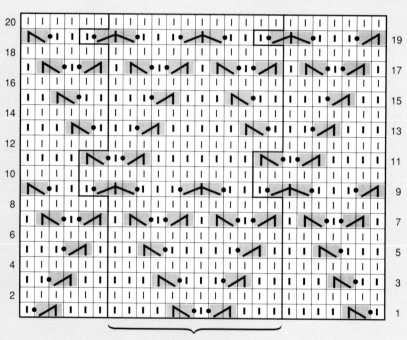

Rep these 12 sts

7th row: *K1, k2tog, yf, k1, yf, sl 1, k1, psso; rep from * to last st, k1.

9th row: K2tog, yf, k3, *yf, sl 1, k2tog, psso, yf, k3; rep from * to last 2 sts, yf, sl 1, k1, psso.

11th row: K4, k2tog, yf, k1, yf, sl 1, k1, psso, *k7, k2tog, yf, k1, yf, sl 1, k1, psso; rep from * to last 4 sts, k4.

13th row: K3, k2tog, yf, k3, yf, sl 1, k1, psso, *k5, k2tog, yf, k3, yf, sl 1, k1, psso; rep from * to last 3 sts, k3.

15th row: K2, k2tog, yf, k5, yf, sl 1, k1, psso, *k3, k2tog, yf, k5, yf, sl 1, k1, psso; rep from * to last 2 sts, k2.

17th row: As 7th row.

19th row: As 9th row.

20th row: Purl.

Rep these 20 rows.

Large All-over Lace Patterns

Fancy Horseshoe Print

Multiple of 10 sts + 11.

1st row (right side): K1, *yf, k3, sl 1, k2tog, psso, k3, yf, k1; rep from * to end.

2nd row: Purl.

3rd row: K2, yf, k2, sl 1, k2tog, psso, k2, *yf, k3, yf, k2, sl 1, k2tog, psso, k2; rep from * to last 2 sts, yf, k2.

4th row: Purl.

5th row: K2tog, [yf, k1] twice, *sl 1, k2tog, psso, [k1, yf] twice, sl 1, k2tog, psso, [yf, k1] twice; rep from * to last 7

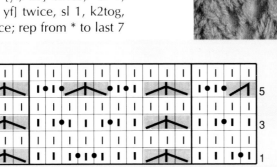

Rep these 10 sts

sts, sl 1, k2tog, psso, [k1, yf] twice, sl 1, k1, psso.

6th row: Purl.

Rep these 6 rows.

Goblet Lace

9th row: K2, yf, sl 1, k1, psso, k3, k2tog, yf, *k3, yf, sl 1, k1, psso, k3, k2tog, yf; rep from * to last 2 sts, k2.

11th row: K3, yf, sl 1, k1, psso, k1, k2tog, yf, *k5, yf, sl 1, k1, psso, k1, k2tog, yf; rep from * to last 3 sts, k3.

13th row: K4, yf, sl 1, k2tog, psso, yf, *k7, yf, sl 1, k2tog, psso, yf; rep from * to last 4 sts, k4.

14th row: Purl.

Rep these 14 rows.

Goblet Lace

Multiple of 10 sts + 1.

1st row (right side): K1, *yf, sl 1, k1, psso, k2tog, yf, k1; rep from * to end.

2nd and every alt row: Purl.

3rd to 6th rows: Rep 1st and 2nd rows twice more.

7th row: K1, *yf, sl 1, k1, psso, k5, k2tog, yf, k1; rep from * to end.

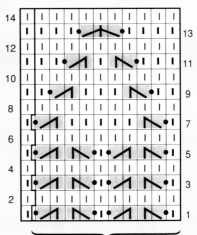

Rep these 10 sts

47

Large All-over Lace Patterns

Eyelet Boxes

Multiple of 14 sts + 9.

1st row (right side): K1, p7, *k3, yf, sl 1, k1, psso, k2, p7; rep from * to last st, k1.

2nd, 4th, 6th, 8th and 10th rows: P1, k7, *p7, k7; rep from * to last st, p1.

3rd row: K1, p7, *k1, k2tog, yf, k1, yf, sl 1, k1, psso, k1, p7; rep from * to last st, k1.

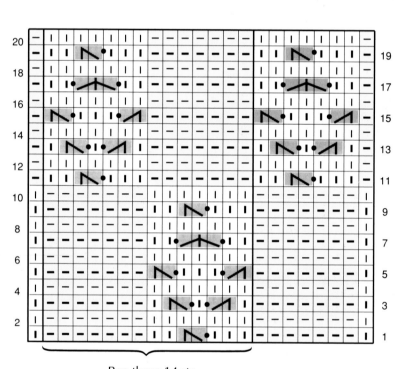

Rep these 14 sts

5th row: K1, p7, *k2tog, yf, k3, yf, sl 1, k1, psso, p7; rep from * to last st, k1.

7th row: K1, p7, *k2, yf, sl 1, k2tog, psso, yf, k2, p7; rep from * to last st, k1.

9th row: As 1st row.

11th row: P1, k3, yf, sl 1, k1, psso, k2, *p7, k3, yf, sl 1, k1, psso, k2; rep from * to last st, p1.

12th, 14th, 16th and 18th rows: K1, p7, *k7, p7; rep from * to last st, k1.

13th row: P1, k1, k2tog, yf, k1, yf, sl 1, k1, psso, k1, *p7, k1, k2tog, yf, k1, yf, sl 1, k1,

psso, k1; rep from * to last st, p1.

15th row: P1, k2tog, yf, k3, yf, sl 1, k1, psso, *p7, k2tog, yf, k3, yf, sl 1, k1, psso; rep from * to last st, p1.

17th row: P1, k2, yf, sl 1, k2tog, psso, yf, k2, *p7, k2, yf, sl 1, k2tog, psso, yf, k2; rep from * to last st, p1.

19th row: As 11th row.

20th row: K1, p7, *k7, p7; rep from * to last st, k1.

Rep these 20 rows.

48

Eyelet Diamonds

Multiple of 16 sts + 11.

1st row (right side): K10, yf, sl 1, k1, psso, k3, k2tog, yf, *k9, yf, sl 1, k1, psso, k3, k2tog, yf; rep from * to last 10 sts, k10.

2nd and every alt row: Purl.

3rd row: K3, k2tog, yf, k1, yf, sl 1, k1, psso, *k3, yf, sl 1, k1, psso, k1, k2tog, yf, k3, k2tog, yf, k1, yf, sl 1, k1, psso; rep from * to last 3 sts, k3.

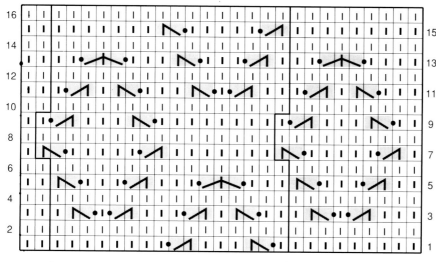

Rep these 16 sts

5th row: K2, k2tog, yf, k3, yf, sl 1, k1, psso, *k3, yf, sl 1, k2tog, psso, yf, k3, k2tog, yf, k3, yf, sl 1, k1, psso; rep from * to last 2 sts, k2.

7th row: K1, k2tog, yf, k5, yf, sl 1, k1, psso, *k7, k2tog, yf, k5, yf, sl 1, k1, psso; rep from * to last st, k1.

9th row: K2, yf, sl 1, k1, psso, k3, k2tog, yf, *k9, yf, sl 1, k1, psso, k3, k2tog, yf; rep from * to last 2 sts, k2.

11th row: K3, yf, sl 1, k1, psso, k1, k2tog, yf, k3, *k2tog, yf, k1, yf, sl 1, k1, psso, k3,

yf, sl 1, k1, psso, k1, k2tog, yf, k3; rep from * to end.

13th row: K4, yf, sl 1, k2tog, psso, yf, *k3, k2tog, yf, k3, yf, sl 1, k1, psso, k3, yf, sl 1, k2tog, psso, yf; rep from * to last 4 sts, k4.

15th row: K9, k2tog, yf, k5, yf, sl 1, k1, psso, *k7, k2tog, yf, k5, yf, sl 1, k1, psso; rep from * to last 9 sts, k9.

16th row: Purl.

Rep these 16 rows.

Small All-over Lace Patterns

Snowflakes

Cast on a multiple of 6 sts + 7.

Note: Do not count sts after 3rd, 4th, 9th or 10th rows.

1st row (right side): K1, *yf, sl 1, k1, psso, k1, k2tog, yf, k1; rep from * to end.

2nd and every alt row: Purl.

3rd row: K2, yf, *k3, yf; rep from * to last 2 sts, k2.

5th row: K2tog, yf, sl 1, k1, psso, k1, k2tog, yf, *sl 1, k2tog, psso, yf, sl 1, k1, psso, k1, k2tog, yf; rep from * to last 2 sts, sl 1, k1, psso.

7th row: K1, *k2tog, yf, k1, yf, sl 1, k1, psso, k1; rep from * to end.

9th row: As 3rd row.

11th row: K1, *k2tog, yf, sl 1, k2tog, psso, yf, sl 1, k1, psso, k1; rep from * to end.

12th row: Purl.

Rep these 12 rows.

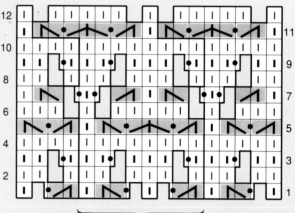

Rep these sts

Snowdrop Lace

Multiple of 8 sts + 5.

1st row (right side): K1, *yf, sl 1, k2tog, psso, yf, k5; rep from * to last 4 sts, yf, sl 1, k2tog, psso, yf, k1.

2nd row: Purl.

3rd and 4th rows: Rep 1st and 2nd rows once more.

5th row: K4, *yf, sl 1, k1, psso, k1, k2tog, yf, k3; rep from * to last st, k1.

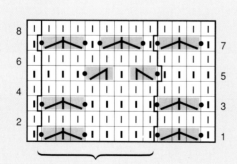

Rep these 8 sts

6th row: Purl.

7th row: K1, *yf, sl 1, k2tog, psso, yf, k1; rep from * to end.

8th row: Purl.

Rep these 8 rows.

Small All-over Lace Patterns

Openwork and Twist Pattern

Multiple of 15 sts + 12.

Special Abbreviation

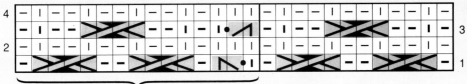 **T4PR (Twist 4 Purl Right)** = slip next 3 sts on to cable needle and hold at back of work, knit next st from left-hand needle, slip the 2 purl sts from cable needle back on to left-hand needle, bring remaining st on cable needle to front of work, purl next 2 sts from left-hand needle, then knit st from cable needle.

1st row (right side): P1, T4PR, p2, T4PR, p1, *k1, yf, sl 1, k1, psso, k1, T4PR, p2, T4PR, p1;

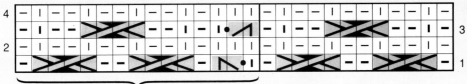

Rep these 15 sts

rep from * to end.

2nd row: K1, p1, [k2, p1] 3 times, k1, *p3, k1, p1, [k2, p1] 3 times, k1; rep from * to end.

3rd row: P1, k1, p2, T4PR, p2, k1, p1, *k2tog, yf, k1, p1, k1, p2, T4PR, p2, k1, p1; rep from * to end.

4th row: As 2nd row.

Rep these 4 rows.

Cell Stitch

Multiple of 4 sts + 7.

Note: Slip sts purlwise.

1st row (right side): K2, *yf, sl 1, k2tog, psso, yf, k1; rep from * to last st, k1.

2nd row: Purl.

3rd row: K1, k2tog, yf, k1, *yf, sl 1, k2tog, psso, yf, k1; rep from * to last 3 sts, yf, sl 1, k1, psso, k1.

4th row: Purl.

Rep these 4 rows.

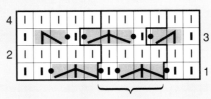

Rep these 4 sts

Lace Panels

Ostrich Plume Panel

Panel of 13 sts on a background of reverse st st.

1st row (right side): K13.

2nd row: P13.

3rd row: K4tog, [yf, k1] 5 times, yf, k4tog.

4th row: P13.

Rep these 4 rows.

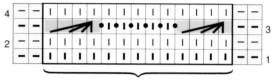

13 sts

Pyramid Panel

Panel of 17 sts on a background of st st.

1st row (right side): [K1, yf, sl 1, k1, psso] twice, p5, [k2tog, yf, k1] twice.

2nd row: P6, k5, p6.

3rd row: K2, yf, sl 1, k1 psso, k1, yf, sl 1, k1, psso, p3, k2tog, yf, k1, k2tog, yf, k2.

4th row: P7, k3, p7.

5th row: K3, yf, sl 1, k1, psso, k1, yf, sl 1, k1, psso, p1, k2tog, yf, k1, k2tog, yf, k3.

6th row: P8, k1, p8.

7th row: K4, yf, sl 1, k1, psso, k1, yf, sl 1, k2tog, psso, yf, k1, k2tog, yf, k4.

8th row: P17.

9th row: K5, yf, sl 1, k1, psso, k3, k2tog, yf, k5.

10th row: P17.

11th row: K6, yf, sl 1, k1, psso, k1, k2tog, yf, k6.

12th row: P17.

13th row: K7, yf, sl 1, k2tog, psso, yf, k7.

14th row: P17.

Rep these 14 rows.

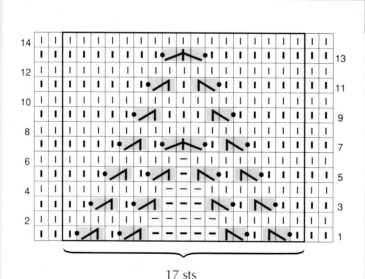

17 sts

Braided Lace Panel

Panel of 20 sts on a background of st st.

1st and every alt row (wrong side): P20.

2nd row: K4, [yf, sl 1, k1, psso] twice, k3, [k2tog, yf] twice, k5.

4th row: K2, [k2tog, yf] twice, k4, [k2tog, yf] twice, k1, yf, sl 1, k1, psso, k3.

6th row: K1, [k2tog, yf] twice, k4, [k2tog, yf] twice, k1, [yf, sl 1, k1, psso] twice, k2.

8th row: [K2tog, yf] twice, k4, [k2tog, yf] twice, k3, [yf, sl 1, k1, psso] twice, k1.

10th row: K2, [yf, sl 1, k1, psso] twice, k1, [k2tog, yf] twice, k5, [yf, sl 1, k1, psso] twice.

12th row: K3, yf, sl 1, k1, psso, yf, sl 1, k2tog, psso, yf, k2tog, yf, k4, [k2tog, yf] twice, k2.

14th row: K4, yf, sl 1, k1, psso, yf, sl 1, k2tog, psso, yf, k4, [k2tog, yf] twice, k3.

16th row: K5, [yf, sl 1, k1, psso] twice, k3, [k2tog, yf] twice, k4.

18th row: K3, k2tog, yf, k1, [yf, sl 1, k1, psso] twice, k4, [yf, sl 1, k1, psso] twice, k2.

20th row: K2, [k2tog, yf] twice, k1, [yf, sl 1, k1, psso] twice, k4, [yf, sl 1, k1, psso] twice, k1.

22nd row: K1, [k2tog, yf] twice, k3, [yf, sl 1, k1, psso] twice, k4, [yf, sl 1, k1, psso] twice.

24th row: [K2tog, yf] twice, k5, [yf, sl 1, k1, psso] twice, k1, [k2tog, yf] twice, k2.

26th row: K2, [yf, sl 1, k1, psso] twice, k4, yf, sl 1, k1, psso, yf, k3tog, yf, k2tog, yf, k3.

28th row: K3, [yf, sl 1, k1, psso] twice, k4, yf, k3tog, yf, k2tog, yf, k4.

Rep these 28 rows.

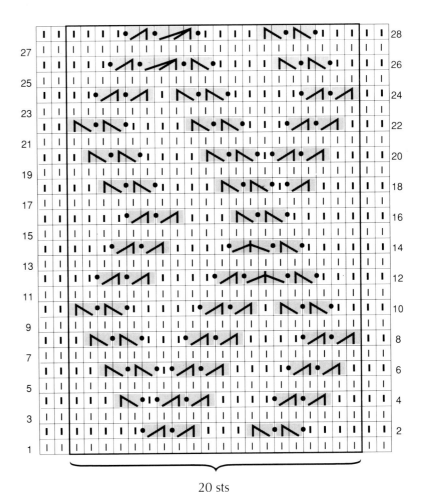

20 sts

Cable and Bobble Sweaters

Measurements

To fit bust size	75/80	85/90	95/100	cm
	30/32	34/36	38/40	ins
Finished measurement	99	111	124	cm
	39½	44½	49½	ins

Length to shoulder (approximately)

Tunic	66	67	67	cm
	26½	26¾	26¾	ins
Sweater	55	57	57	cm
	22	22¾	22¾	ins

Sleeve length (approximately)

Tunic	45	46	46	cm
	18	18½	18½	ins
Sweater	15	16	16	cm
	6	6½	6½	ins

Both garments shown in 85/90 cm [34/36 inch] size.

Materials

Cotton Double Knitting yarn

Tunic

Main Colour (M)	600	700	750	grams
	22	25	27	ounces
Contrast Colour (C)	100	100	100	grams
	4	4	4	ounces

Sweater

	450	500	600	grams
	16	18	22	ounces

Pair needles each size 3¼mm (UK 10, USA 3 or 4) and 4mm (UK 8, USA 6).
Cable needle.

The quantities of yarn stated are based on average requirements and are therefore approximate.

For abbreviations see pages 18 and 19.

Tension

22 sts and 30 rows = 10 cm [4 ins] square measured over st st using larger needles.

Special Abbreviations

MB (Make Bobble) = [k1, yf, k1, yf, k1] in next st, turn, p5, turn, k5, turn, p2tog, p1, p2tog, turn, sl 1, k2tog, psso (bobble completed).

MC (Make Cluster) = [sl 1] 5 times, yb, [sl 1] 5 times back to left-hand needle, yf, [sl 1] 5 times.

Note: Where a number of sts is given, this refers to the basic number and does not include those made in the pattern.

Panel A (4 sts)

1st row (right side): K2, k2tog, yfrn.

2nd row: Purl.

3rd row: K1, k2tog, yf, k1.

4th row: Purl.

5th row: K2tog, yf, k2.

6th row: Purl.

These 6 rows form panel A.

Panel B (17 sts)

1st row (right side): Knit.

2nd row: [P1, k3] 4s times, p1.

3rd row: Yon, k17, yfrn.

4th row: P2, [k3, p1] 4 times, p1.

5th row: K1, yf, k1,[k2tog, k2] 4 times, yf, k1.

6th row: P3, [k2, p1] 4 times, p2.

7th row: K2, yf, k13, yf, k2.

8th row: P4, [k2, p1] 4 times, p3.

9th row: K3, yf, [k1, k2tog] 4 times, k1, yf, k3.

10th row: P5, [k1, p1] 4 times, p4.

11th row: K4, yf, k9, yf, k4.

12th row: P6, [k1, p1] 4 times, p5.

13th row: K5, yf, [sl 1, k1, psso] twice, k1, [k2tog] twice, yf, k5.

14th row: P6, MC, p6.

These 14 rows form panel B.

Panel C (22 sts)

1st row (right side): [P3, k2] twice, p2, [k2, p3] twice.

2nd row: [K3, p2] twice, k2, [p2, k3] twice.

3rd row: P3, T3F, p2, T3F, T3B, p2, T3B, p3.

4th row: K4, p2, k3, p4, k3, p2, k4.

5th row: P4, T3F, p2, C4F, p2, T3B, p4.

6th row: K5, p2, k2, p4, k2, p2, k5.

7th row: P5, [T3F, T3B] twice, p5.

8th row: K6, p4, k2, p4, k6.

9th row: P6, C4F, p2, C4F, p6.

10th row: As 8th row.

11th row: P5, [T3B, T3F] twice, p5.

12th row: As 6th row.

13th row: P4, T3B, p2, C4F, p2, T3F, p4.

14th row: As 4th row.

15th row: P3, T3B, p2, T3B, T3F, p2, T3F, p3.

16th row: As 2nd row.

17th to 20th rows: As 1st to 4th rows.

21st row: P4, T3F, p2, C4B, p2, T3B, p4.

Cable and Bobble Sweaters

22nd to 24th rows: As 6th to 8th rows.

25th row: P6, C4B, p2, C4B, p6.

26th to 28th rows: As 10th to 12th rows.

29th row: P4, T3B, p2, C4B, p2, T3F, p4.

30th to 32nd rows: As 14th to 16th rows.

These 32 rows form panel C.

Tunic

Back

Using larger needles and C, cast on 165(185-205) sts.

1st row (wrong side): Knit.

2nd row: Purl.

Break off C. Join in M and purl 1 row.

Commence border pattern.

1st row (right side): Knit.

2nd row: P5, *[k3, p1] 4 times, p4; rep from * to end.

3rd row: K1, *k3tog, yf, k17, yf; rep from * to last 4 sts, k3tog, k1.

4th row: P3, *p1, [k3, p1] 4 times, p3; rep from * to end.

5th row: K2, *k1, yf, k1, [k2tog, k2] 4 times, yf, k2; rep from * to last st, k1. 147(165-183) sts.

6th row: P3, *p2, [k2, p1] 4 times, p4; rep from * to end.

7th row: K1, k3tog, yf, *k13, yf, k1, k3tog, k1, yf; rep from * to last 17 sts, k13, yf, k3tog, k1. 145(163-181) sts.

8th row: P1, *p3, [k2, p1] 4 times, p3; rep from * to end.

9th row: *K3, yf, [k1, k2tog] 4 times, k1, yf, k2; rep from * to last st, k1. 129(145-161) sts.

10th row: P1, *p4, [k1, p1] 4 times, p4; rep from * to end.

11th row: K1, k3tog, *yf, k9, yf, k2, k3tog, k2; rep from * to last 13 sts, yf, k9, yf, k3tog, k1. 127(143-159) sts.

12th row: P4, *[k1, p1] 4 times, p8; rep from * to last 11 sts, [k1, p1] 4 times, p3.

13th row: K3, *yf, [sl 1, k1, psso] twice, k1, [k2tog] twice, yf, k7; rep from * to last 12 sts, yf, [sl 1, k1, psso] twice, k1, [k2tog] twice, yf, k3. 111(125-139) sts.

14th row: P4, *MC, p9; rep from * to last 9 sts, MC, p2, p2tog. 110(124-138) sts.

★ Commence main pattern.

1st row (right side): P3(4-5), [work 1st row of panel A across next 4 sts, p2] 1(2-3) times, work 1st row of panel B across next 17 sts, [p2, work 1st row of panel A across next 4 sts] 3 times, work 1st row of panel C across next 22 sts, [work 1st row of panel A across next 4 sts, p2] 3 times, work 1st row of panel B across next 17 sts, [p2, work 1st row of panel A across next 4 sts] 1(2-3) times, p3(4-5).

2nd row: K3(4-5), [work 2nd row of panel A, k2] 1(2-3) times, work 2nd row of panel B, [k2, work 2nd row of panel A] 3 times, work 2nd row of panel C, [work 2nd row of panel A, k2], 3 times, work 2nd row of panel B, [k2, work 2nd row of panel A] 1(2-3) times, k3(4-5).

These 2 rows set the positon of panels and form reverse st st at each side and between panels ★.

Continue in pattern as set, **working appropriate rows of panels**, until 174 rows in all have been worked, thus ending with wrong side row.

★★ Shape Neck

Next row: Work 35(42-49) sts in pattern, turn and complete this side first.

Keeping pattern correct, cast off 0(3-3) sts at beg of next row, then dec 1 st at neck edge on next 2(5-5) rows. 33(34-41) sts remain.

Work 4(3-3) rows, thus ending at side edge. Cast off.

With right side of work facing, slip centre 40 sts on to a holder, rejoin yarn to remaining 35(42-49) sts, work in pattern to end. Complete to match first side, reversing shapings.

Front

Work as given for Back until front is 32(36-36) rows shorter than back to shoulder, thus ending with a wrong side row.

★★★ Shape Neck

Next row: Work 43(47-54) sts in pattern, turn and complete this side first.

Keeping pattern correct, dec 1 st at neck edge on next 4 rows, then on following 6(9-9) alt rows. 33(34-41) sts remain.

Work 15(13-13) rows, thus ending with a wrong side row. Cast off.

With right side of work facing, slip centre 24(30-30) sts on to a holder, rejoin yarn to remaining 43(47-54) sts, work in pattern to end. Complete to match first side, reversing shapings.

Sleeves

Using smaller needles and C, cast on 47 sts.

1st row (wrong side): Knit.

2nd row: P2, *MB, p6; rep from * to last 3 sts, MB, p2.

Break off C. Join in M, purl 1 row and work in rib as follows:

1st row (right side): K1, *p1, k1; rep from * to end.

2nd row: P1, *k1, p1; rep from * to end.

Rep these 2 rows 4(5-5) times more.

Break off M. Join in C and work 2

Cable and Bobble Sweaters

rows in garter st (every row knit).

Next row: P2, *MB, p6; rep from * to last 3 sts, MB, p2.

Break off C. Join in M.

Next row (increase): P1, *inc in next st, p1; rep from * to end. 70 sts.

Change to larger needles and commence pattern.

1st row (right side): [P2, work 1st row of panel A across next 4 sts] 4 times, work 1st row of panel C across next 22 sts, [work 1st row of panel A across next 4 sts, p2] 4 times.

2nd row: [K2, work 2nd row of panel A] 4 times, work 2nd row of panel C, [work 2nd row of panel A, k2] 4 times.

These 2 rows set the position of panels and form reverse st st at each side and between panels.

Continue in pattern as set, **working appropriate rows of panels** and bringing extra sts into panel A, inc 1 st at each end of 9th(7th-5th) row (from beg of pattern) and every following 8th(6th-4th) row until there are 80(102-100) sts, then on every

following 10th(8th-6th) row until there are 94(106-118) sts. Work 9(7-5) rows, thus ending with a wrong side row. Cast off **loosely**.

Finishing and Neckband

Block but do not press.

Using C and chain stitch, embroider on border as in photograph.

Join right shoulder seam.

Neckband

With right side of work facing, using smaller needles and C, pick up and k30(32-32) sts down left front slope, work across 24(30-30) sts from centre front as follows: k3(1-1), [k2tog, k3] 3(5-5) times, k2tog, k4(2-2), pick up and knit 30(32-32) sts up right front slope, 5(8-8) sts down right back slope, work across 40 sts from centre back as follows: k3, [k2tog, k2] 8 times, k2tog, k3, then pick up and k5(8-8) sts up left back slope. 121(135-135) sts.

Next row (wrong side): Knit.

Next row: P4(3-3), *MB, p7; rep from * to last 5(4-4) sts, MB, purl to end.

Break off C. Join in M and purl 1 row, then work 10(12-12) rows in k1, p1 rib as given for Sleeves.

Break off M. Join in C.

Next row (decrease): K1(0-0), k2tog, *k3, k2tog, k1, k2tog; rep from * to last 6(5-5) sts, k3, k2tog, k1(0-0). 91(101-101) sts.

Next row: Knit.

Next row: P3(2-2), *MB, p5; rep from * to last 4(3-3) sts, MB, purl to end.

Cast off purlwise.

Join left shoulder seam and ends of neckband. Fold each sleeve in half lengthways and mark centre of cast off edge. Sew each sleeve to a side edge placing centre at shoulder seam. Join side and sleeve seams.

Sweater

Back

Using smaller needles, cast on 85(95-107) sts.

1st row (wrong side): Knit.

2nd row: P7(5-4), *MB, p6; rep from * to last 8(6-5) sts, MB, p7(5-4).

Purl 1 row, then work 10(12-12) rows in k1, p1 rib as given for Sleeves of Tunic.

Next row: P7(5-4), *MB, p6; rep from * to last 8(6-5) sts, MB, p7(5-4).

Next row (increase): P6(5-8), *inc in next st, p2; rep from * to last 7(6-9) sts, inc in next st, purl to end. 110(124-138) sts.

Change to larger needles and work as given for Back of Tunic from ★ to ★.

Continue in pattern as set, **working appropriate rows of panels**, until 146 rows in all have been worked, thus ending with a wrong side row.

Work as given for Back of Tunic from ★★ to end.

Front

Work as given for Back until front is 32(36-36) rows shorter than back to shoulder, thus ending with a wrong side row.

Cable and Bobble Sweater

Work as given for Front of Tunic from ★★★ to end.

Sleeves

Using smaller needles, cast on 55(67-77) sts.

1st row (wrong side): Knit.

2nd row: P3(3-2), *MB, p5; rep from * to last 4(4-3) sts, MB, purl to end.

Purl 1 row, then work 10(12-12) rows in k1, p1 rib as given for Sleeves of Tunic.

Next row: P3(3-2), *MB, p5; rep from * to last 4(4-3) sts, MB, purl to end.

Next row (increase): P1(7-10), *inc in next st, p1; rep from * to last 2(8-11) sts, inc in next st, purl to end. 82(94-106) sts.

Change to larger needles and commnence pattern.

1st row (right side): [P2, work 1st row of panel A across next 4 sts] 5(6-7) times, work 1st row of panel C across next 22 sts, [work 1st row of panel A across next 4 sts, p2] 5(6-7) times.

2nd row: [K2, work 2nd row of panel A] 5(6-7) times, work 2nd row of panel C, [work 2nd row of panel A, k2] 5(6-7) times.

These 2 rows set the position of panels and form reverse st st at each side and between panels.

Continue in pattern as set, **working appropriate rows of panels** and bringing extra sts into panel A, inc 1 st at each end of 5th row (from beg of pattern) and every following 4th row until there are 94(106-118) sts. Work 5 rows straight, thus ending with a wrong side row. Cast off **loosely**.

Finishing and Neckband

Block but do not press.

Complete as given for Tunic omitting embroidery and using one colour throughout.

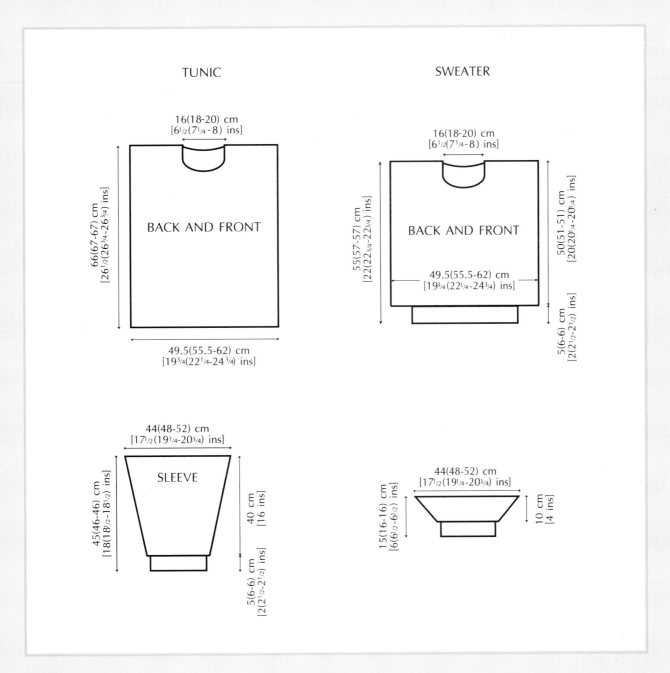

TUNIC

16(18-20) cm
[6½(7¼ - 8) ins]

BACK AND FRONT

66(67-67) cm
[26½(26¾-26¾) ins]

49.5(55.5-62) cm
[19¾(22¼-24¾) ins]

SWEATER

16(18-20) cm
[6½(7¼ - 8) ins]

BACK AND FRONT

55(57-57) cm
[22(22¾-22¾) ins]

49.5(55.5-62) cm
[19¾(22¼-24¾) ins]

50(51-51) cm
[20(20¼-20¼) ins]

5(6-6) cm
[2(2½-2½) ins]

44(48-52) cm
[17½(19¼-20¾) ins]

SLEEVE

45(46-46) cm
[18(18½-18½) ins]

40 cm
[16 ins]

5(6-6) cm
[2(2½-2½) ins]

44(48-52) cm
[17½(19¼-20¾) ins]

15(16-16) cm
[6(6½-6½) ins]

10 cm
[4 ins]

All-over Bobble and Lace Pattern

Open Diamonds with Bobbles

Multiple of 10 sts + 11.

Special Abbreviation

● **MB (Make Bobble)** = [k1, p1, k1, p1, k1] into next st, turn and k5, turn and p5, turn and sl 1, k1, psso, k1, k2tog, turn and p3tog (bobble completed).

1st row (right side): P1, *yon, sl 1, k1, psso, p5, k2tog, yfrn, p1; rep from * to end.

2nd row: K2, *p1, k5, p1, k3; rep from * to last 9 sts, p1, k5, p1, k2.

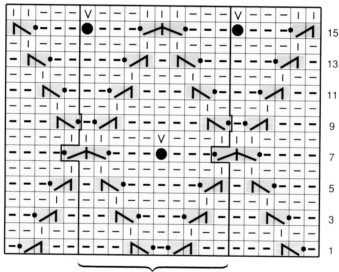

Rep these 10 sts

3rd row: P2, *yon, sl 1, k1, psso, p3, k2tog, yfrn, p3; rep from * to last 9 sts, yon, sl 1, k1, psso, p3, k2tog, yfrn, p2.

4th row: K3, *p1, k3, p1, k5; rep from * to last 8 sts, [p1, k3] twice.

5th row: P3, *yon, sl 1, k1, psso, p1, k2tog, yfrn, p5; rep from * to last 8 sts, yon, sl 1, k1, psso, p1, k2tog, yfrn, p3.

6th row: K4, *p1, k1, p1, k7; rep from * to last 7 sts, p1, k1, p1, k4.

7th row: P4, *yon, sl 1, k2tog, psso, yfrn, p3, MB, p3; rep from * to last 7 sts, yon, sl 1, k2tog, psso, yfrn, p4.

8th row: K4, *p3, k3, PB1, k3; rep from * to last 7 sts, p3, k4.

9th row: P3, *k2tog, yfrn, p1, yon, sl 1, k1, psso, p5; rep from * to last 8 sts, k2tog, yfrn, p1, yon, sl 1, k1, psso, p3.

10th row: As 4th row.

11th row: P2, *k2tog, yfrn, p3, yon, sl 1, k1, psso, p3; rep from * to last 9 sts, k2tog, yfrn, p3, yon, sl 1, k1, psso, p2.

12th row: As 2nd row.

13th row: P1, *k2tog, yfrn, p5, yon, sl 1, k1, psso, p1; rep from * to end.

14th row: K1, *p1, k7, p1, k1; rep from * to end.

15th row: K2tog, *yfrn, p3, MB, p3, yon, sl 1, k2tog, psso; rep from * to last 9 sts, yfrn, p3, MB, p3, yon, sl 1, k1, psso.

16th row: P2, *k3, PB1, k3, p3; rep from * to last 9 sts, k3, PB1, k3, p2.

Rep these 16 rows.

Bobble and Lace Panel

Bobble Spray Panel

Panel of 23 sts on a background of st st.

Special Abbreviation

● **MB (Make Bobble)** = knit into front, back and front of next st, turn and k3, turn and p3, turn and k3, turn and sl 1, k2tog, psso (bobble completed).

1st row (right side): Sl 1, k1, psso, k6, [yf, k1] twice, sl 1, k2tog, psso, [k1, yf] twice, k6, k2tog.

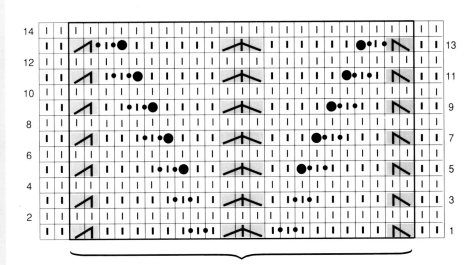

23 sts

2nd and every alt row: Purl.

3rd row: Sl 1, k1, psso, k5, yf, k1, yf, k2, sl 1, k2tog, psso, k2, yf, k1, yf, k5, k2tog.

5th row: Sl 1, k1, psso, k4, yf, k1, yf, MB, k2, sl 1, k2tog, psso, k2, MB, yf, k1, yf, k4, k2tog.

7th row: Sl 1, k1, psso, k3, yf, k1, yf, MB, k3, sl 1, k2tog, psso, k3, MB, yf, k1, yf, k3, k2tog.

9th row: Sl 1, k1, psso, k2, yf, k1, yf, MB, k4, sl 1, k2tog, psso, k4, MB, yf, k1, yf, k2, k2tog.

11th row: Sl 1, k1, psso, [k1, yf] twice, MB, k5, sl 1, k2tog, psso, k5, MB, [yf, k1] twice, k2tog.

13th row: Sl 1, k1, psso, yf, k1, yf, MB, k6, sl 1, k2tog, psso, k6, MB, yf, k1, yf, k2tog.

14th row: Purl.

Rep these 14 rows.

All-over Bobble Patterns

1st row (right side): P2, *C2F, p2; rep from * to end.

2nd row: K2, *p2, k2; rep from * to end.

3rd row: P2, k1, MB, p2, *C2F, p2, k1, MB, p2; rep from * to end.

4th row: As 2nd row.

5th and 6th rows: As 1st and 2nd rows.

7th row: P2, C2F, p2, *k1, MB, p2, C2F, p2; rep from * to end.

8th row: As 2nd row.

Rep these 8 rows.

Bobble Twists

Multiple of 8 sts + 6.

Special Abbreviation

● **MB (Make Bobble)** = [k1, yf, k1, yf, k1] into next st, turn, p5, turn, k5, turn, p2tog, p1, p2tog, turn, sl 1, k2tog, psso (bobble completed).

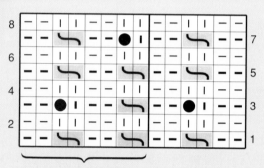

Rep these 8 sts

Bobble and Ridge Stitch

Multiple of 6 sts + 5.

Special Abbreviation

● **MB (Make Bobble)** = knit into front, back and front of next st, turn and p3, turn and k3, turn and p3, turn and sl 1, k2tog, psso (bobble completed).

1st row (right side): Knit.

2nd row: Purl.

3rd row: K5, *MB, k5; rep from * to end.

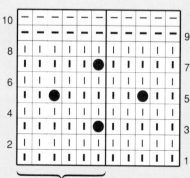

Rep these 6 sts

4th row: Purl.

5th row: K2, MB, *k5, MB; rep from * to last 2 sts, k2.

6th to 8th rows: As 2nd to 4th rows.

9th row: Purl.

10th row: Knit.

Rep these 10 rows.

All-over Bobble Patterns

Bobbles

Multiple of 10 sts + 5.

Special Abbreviation

● **MB (Make Bobble)** = knit into front, back and front of next st, turn and k3, turn and p3, turn and k3, turn and sl 1, k2tog, psso (bobble completed).

1st row (right side): Knit.

2nd row: Purl.

3rd and 4th rows: Rep 1st and 2nd rows once more.

5th row: K7, *MB, k9; rep from * to last 8 sts, MB, k7.

6th row: Purl.

7th to 10th rows: Rep 1st and 2nd rows twice.

11th row: K2, *MB, k9; rep from * to last 3 sts, MB, k2.

12th row: Purl.

Rep these 12 rows.

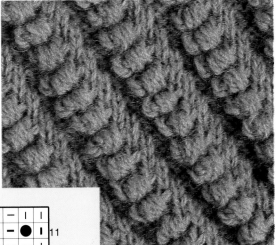

Rep these 10 sts

Diagonal Bobble Stitch

Multiple of 6 sts + 6.

Special Abbreviation

● **MB (Make Bobble)** = [knit into front and back] 3 times into next st, pass 2nd, 3rd, 4th, 5th and 6th sts over first st and off needle.

1st row (right side): *K2, MB, p3; rep from * to end.

2nd row: *K3, p3; rep from * to end.

3rd row: P1, *k2, MB, p3; rep from * to last 5 sts, k2, MB, p2.

4th row: K2, *p3, k3; rep from * to last 4 sts, p3, k1.

5th row: P2, *k2, MB, p3; rep from * to last 4 sts, k2, MB, p1.

6th row: K1, *p3, k3; rep from * to last 5 sts, p3, k2.

7th row: *P3, k2, MB; rep from * to end.

8th row: *P3, k3; rep from * to end.

9th row: *MB, p3, k2; rep from

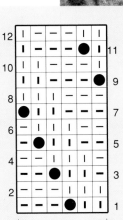

Rep these 6 sts

* to end.

10th row: P2, *k3, p3; rep from * to last 4 sts, k3, p1.

11th row: K1, *MB, p3, k2; rep from * to last 5 sts, MB, p3, k1.

12th row: P1, *k3, p3; rep from * to last 5 sts, k3, p2.

Rep these 12 rows.

Bobble Panels

1st row (right side): K2, C2F, k2, C2B, k5.

2nd and every alt row: P13.

3rd row: K3, C2F, C2B, k6.

5th row: K4, C2F, k4, MB, k2.

7th row: K5, C2F, k2, C2B, k2.

9th row: K6, C2F, C2B, k3.

11th row: K2, MB, k4, C2B, k4.

12th row: P13.

Rep these 12 rows.

Branched Grapevine Panel

Panel of 13 sts on a background of reverse st st.

Special Abbreviation

● **MB (Make Bobble)** = [k1, yf, k1, yf, k1] into next st, turn and k5, turn and p5, turn and k1, sl 1, k2tog, psso, k1, turn and p3tog (bobble completed).

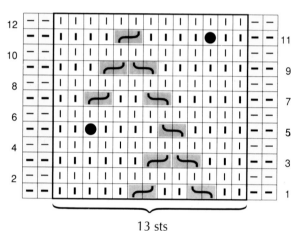

13 sts

Bobble Tree

Panel of 12 sts on a background of reverse st st.

Special Abbreviation

● **MB (Make Bobble)** = knit into front, back and front of next st, turn and k3, turn and p3, turn and k3, turn and sl 1, k2tog, psso (bobble completed).

1st row (wrong side): K5, p2, k5.

2nd row: P4, C2B, C2F, p4.

3rd row: K3, T2FW, p2, T2BW, k3.

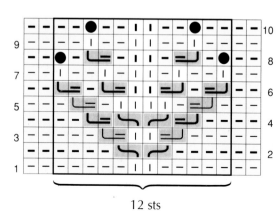

12 sts

4th row: P2, T2B, C2B, C2F, T2F, p2.

5th row: K1, T2FW, k1, p4, k1, T2BW, k1.

6th row: T2B, p1, T2B, k2, T2F, p1, T2F.

7th row: P1, k2, p1, k1, p2, k1, p1, k2, p1.

8th row: MB, p1, T2B, p1, k2, p1, T2F, p1, MB.

9th row: K2, p1, k2, p2, k2, p1, k2.

10th row: P2, MB, p2, k2, p2, MB, p2.

Rep these 10 rows.

Bobble and Cable Panels

Moss Stitch Diamonds

Panel of 15 sts on a background of reverse st st.

Special Abbreviation

● **MB (Make Bobble)** = [k1, p1] twice into next st, turn and k4, turn and p4, turn and k4, turn and sl 2, k2tog, p2sso (bobble completed).

1st row (right side): P5, k2, MB, k2, p5.

2nd row: K5, p5, k5.

3rd row: P5, MB, k3, MB, p5.

4th row: K5, p5, k5.

5th and 6th rows: As 1st and 2nd rows.

7th row: P4, C3B, p1, C3F, p4.

8th row: K4, p3, k1, p3, k4.

9th row: P3, C3B, p1, k1, p1, C3F, p3.

10th row: K3, p3, k1, p1, k1, p3, k3.

11th row: P2, C3B, p1, [k1, p1] twice, C3F, p2.

12th row: K2, p3, k1, [p1, k1] twice, p3, k2.

13th row: P1, C3B, p1, [k1, p1] 3 times, C3F, p1.

14th row: K1, p3, k1, [p1, k1] 3 times, p3, k1.

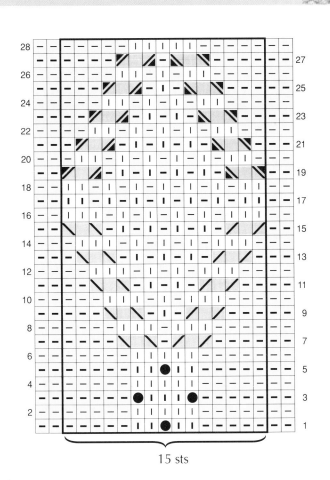

15th row: C3B, p1, [k1, p1] 4 times, C3F.

16th row: P3, k1, [p1, k1] 4 times, p3.

17th row: K2, p1, [k1, p1] 5 times, k2.

18th row: P2, k1, [p1, k1] 5 times, p2.

19th row: T3F, p1, [k1, p1] 4 times, T3B.

20th row: K1, p2, k1, [p1, k1] 4 times, p2, k1.

21st row: P1, T3F, p1, [k1, p1] 3 times, T3B, p1.

22nd row: K2, p2, k1, [p1, k1] 3 times, p2, k2.

23rd row: P2, T3F, p1, [k1, p1] twice, T3B, p2.

24th row: K3, p2, k1, [p1, k1] twice, p2, k3.

25th row: P3, T3F, p1, k1, p1, T3B, p3.

26th row: K4, p2, k1, p1, k1, p2, k4.

27th row: P4, T3F, p1, T3B, p4.

28th row: K5, p5, k5.

Rep these 28 rows.

Bobble and Cable Panels

Bobbles and Waves

Panel of 26 sts on a background of reverse st st.

Special Abbreviation

● **MB (Make Bobble) =** knit into front, back and front of next st, [turn and k3] 3 times, then turn and sl 1, k2tog, psso (bobble completed).

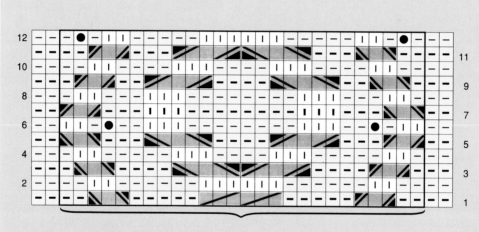

26 sts

1st row (right side): P2, T3B, p5, C6B, p5, T3F, p2.

2nd row: K2, p2, k6, p6, k6, p2, k2.

3rd row: P1, T3B, p4, T5R, T5L, p4, T3F, p1.

4th row: K1, p2, k5, p3, k4, p3, k5, p2, k1.

5th row: T3B, p3, T5R, p4, T5L, p3, T3F.

6th row: P2, k1, MB, k2, p3, k8, p3, k2, MB, k1, p2.

7th row: T3F, p3, k3, p8, k3, p3, T3B.

8th row: K1, p2, k3, p3, k8, p3, k3, p2, k1.

9th row: P1, T3F, p2, T5L, p4, T5R, p2, T3B, p1.

10th row: K2, p2, [k4, p3] twice, k4, p2, k2.

11th row: P2, T3F, p3, T5L, T5R, p3, T3B, p2.

12th row: K1, MB, k1, p2, k5, p6, k5, p2, k1, MB, k1.

Rep these 12 rows.

Bobble and Cable Panels

Moss Stitch Hearts

Panel of 19 sts on a background of reverse st st.

Special Abbreviation

● **MB (Make Bobble)** = knit into front, back and front of next st, turn and k3, turn and p3, turn and k3, turn and sl 1, k2tog, psso (bobble completed).

1st row (right side): P6, T3B, k1, T3F, p6.

2nd row: K6, p3, k1, p3, k6.

3rd row: P5, C3B, p1, k1, p1, C3F, p5.

4th row: K5, p2, [k1, p1] twice, k1, p2, k5.

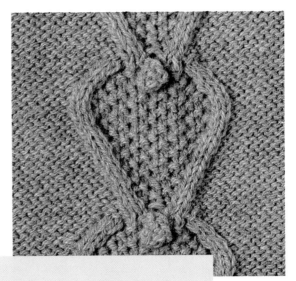

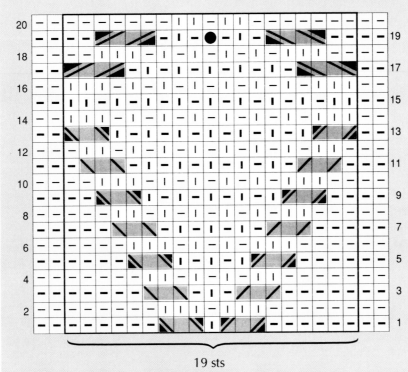

19 sts

5th row: P4, T3B, [k1, p1] twice, k1, T3F, p4.

6th row: K4, p3, [k1, p1] twice, k1, p3, k4.

7th row: P3, C3B, [p1, k1] 3 times, p1, C3F, p3.

8th row: K3, p2, [k1, p1] 4 times, k1, p2, k3.

9th row: P2, T3B, [k1, p1] 4 times, k1, T3F, p2.

10th row: K2, p3, [k1, p1] 4 times, k1, p3, k2.

11th row: P1, C3B, [p1, k1] 5 times, p1, C3F, p1.

12th row: K1, p2, [k1, p1] 6 times, k1, p2, k1.

13th row: T3B, [k1, p1] 6 times, k1, T3F.

14th row: P3, [k1, p1] 6 times, k1, p3.

15th row: K2, [p1, k1] 7 times, p1, k2.

16th row: As 14th row.

17th row: T4F, [p1, k1] 5 times, p1, T4B.

18th row: K2, p3, [k1, p1] 4 times, k1, p3, k2.

19th row: P2, T4F, p1, k1, p1, MB, p1, k1, p1, T4B, p2.

20th row: K7, p2, k1, p2, k7.

Rep these 20 rows.

Mohair Cabled Sweater

Measurements

To fit bust size	80/85	90/95	100/105	cm
	32/34	36/38	40/42	ins
Finished measurement	114	123	134	cm
	45¹/₂	49	53¹/₂	ins
Length to shoulder	71	72	73	cm
	28	28¹/₄	28³/₄	ins
Sleeve length	46	46	47	cm
	18	18	18¹/₂	ins

Shown in 90/95 cm [36/38 inch] size.

Materials

Mohair knitting yarn	750	850	950	grams
	27	31	34	ounces

Pair needles each size 5¹/₂mm (UK 5, USA 9) and 4mm (UK 8, USA 6). Cable needle.

The quantities of yarn stated are based on average requirements and are therefore approximate.

For abbreviations see pages 18 and 19.

Tension

15 sts and 20 rows = 10 cm [4 ins] square measured over st st using larger needles.

28 sts and 21 rows = 10 cm [4 ins] square measured over cable panels A and B using larger needles.

Panel A (12 sts)

1st row (right side): K12.

2nd row: P12.

3rd row: C12B.

4th row: P12.

5th to 12th rows: Rep 1st and 2nd rows 4 times.

These 12 rows form panel A.

Panel B (12 sts)

1st row (right side): K12.

2nd row: P12.

3rd row: C12F.

4th row: P12.

5th to 12th rows: Rep 1st and 2nd rows 4 times.

These 12 rows form panel B.

Panel C (8 sts)

1st row (right side): P2, C4B, p2.

2nd row: K2, p4, k2.

3rd row: P1, T3B, T3F, p1.

4th row: K1, p2, k2, p2, k1.

5th row: T3B, p2, T3F.

6th row: P2, k4, p2.

7th row: K2, p4, k2.

8th row: P2, k4, p2.

9th row: T3F, p2, T3B.

10th row: K1, p2, k2, p2, k1.

11th row: P1, T3F, T3B, p1.

12th row: K2, p4, k2.

These 12 rows form panel C.

Panel D (36 sts)

1st row (right side): C4B, [p4, C4B] 4 times.

2nd row: P4, [k4, p4] 4 times.

3rd row: K2, [T4F, T4B] 4 times, k2.

4th row: P2, k2, [p4, k4] 3 times, p4, k2, p2.

5th row: K2, p2, [C4F, p4] 3 times, C4F, p2, k2.

6th row: As 4th row.

7th row: K2, [T4B, T4F] 4 times, k2.

8th row: As 2nd row.

9th and 10th rows: As 1st and 2nd rows.

11th row: K4, [p2, T4B, T4F, p2, k4] twice.

12th row: P4, [k2, p2, k4, p2, k2, p4] twice.

13th row: C4B, [p2, k2, p4, k2, p2, C4B] twice.

14th row: As 12th row.

15th row: K4, [p2, T4F, T4B, p2, k4] twice.

16th row: As 2nd row.

These 16 rows form panel D.

Back

Using smaller needles cast on 119(129-143) sts.

1st row (right side): K1, *p1, k1; rep from * to end.

2nd row: P1, *k1, p1; rep from * to end.

Rep the last 2 rows until rib measures 4 cm [1¹/₂ ins] ending with a wrong side row.

Next row (increase): Rib 5(1-4), *inc in next st, rib 4(2-2), inc in next st, rib 3; rep from * to last 6(2-6) sts, inc in next st, rib to end. 144(166-182) sts.

Change to larger needles.

Foundation row: K0(3-0), p4(12-0), k4(4-3), [p4, k4, p12, k4] 1(1-2) times, p4, k4, p12, k2, [p4, k4] 4 times, p4, k2, [p12, k4, p4, k4] 1(1-2) times, p12, k4, p4, k4(4-3), p4(12-0), k0(3-0).

Commence pattern.

1st and 3rd sizes only

1st row: K4(0), p2(1), [work 1st row of panel C across next 8 sts, p2, work 1st row of panel A across next 12 sts, p2] 2(3) times, work 1st row of panel D across next 36 sts, [p2, work 1st row of panel B across next 12 sts, p2, work 1st row of panel C across next 8 sts] 2(3) times, p2(1), k4(0).

2nd row: P4(0), k2(1), [work 2nd row of panel C, k2, work 2nd row of panel B, k2] 2(3) times, work 2nd row of panel D, [k2, work 2nd row of panel A, k2, work 2nd row of panel C] 2(3) times, k2(1), p4(0).

2nd size only

1st row: P3, work 1st row of panel A across next 12 sts, p2, [work 1st row of panel C across next 8 sts, p2, work 1st row of panel A across next 12 sts, p2] twice, work 1st row of panel D across next 36 sts, [p2,

Mohair Cabled Sweater

work 1st row of panel B across next 12 sts, p2, work 1st row of panel C across next 8 sts] twice, p2, work 1st row of panel B across next 12 sts, p3.

2nd row: K3, work 2nd row of panel B, k2, [work 2nd row of panel C, k2, work 2nd row of panel B, k2] twice, work 2nd row of panel D, [k2, work 2nd row of panel A, k2, work 2nd row of panel C] twice, k2 work 2nd row of panel A, k3.

All sizes

These 2 rows set the position of cable panels and form reverse st st between. Continue in pattern as set, **working appropriate rows of panels**, until back measures 71(72-73) cm [28(28¼-28¾) ins] ending with a wrong side row.

Shape Shoulders

Cast off 47(57-64) sts at beg of next 2 rows. Cast off remaining 50(52-54) sts for back neck.

Front

Work as given for Back until front is 19 rows shorter than back to start of shoulder shaping, thus ending with a right side row.

Shape Neck

Next row: Work 61(71-78) sts in pattern, turn and complete this side first.

Keeping pattern correct, cast off 4 sts at beg of next row. Cast off 3 sts at beg of following alt row, then 2 sts at beg of following 2 alt rows. Dec 1 st at beg of following 3 alt rows. 47(57-64) sts remain. Work 6 rows straight, thus ending at side edge. Cast off.

With wrong side of work facing, rejoin yarn to next st and cast off centre 22(24-26) sts, work in pattern to end. 61(71-78) sts. Work 1 row straight. Keeping pattern correct, cast off 4 sts at beg of next row. Cast off 3 sts at beg of following alt row, then 2 sts at beg of following 2 alt rows. Dec 1 st at beg of following 3 alt rows. 47(57-64) sts remain. Work 4 rows straight, thus ending at side edge. Cast off.

Sleeves

Note: During shaping, when there are insufficient sts to work a cable twist, work these sts in st st or reverse st st as appropriate.

Using smaller needles cast on 49 sts and work 6 cm [2½ ins] in k1, p1 rib as given for Back ending with a wrong side row.

Next row (increase): Rib 3, *inc in next st, rib 2; rep from * to last 4 sts, inc in next st, rib 3. 64 sts.

Change to larger needles.

Foundation row: K2, [p12, k4, p4, k4] twice, p12, k2.

Commence pattern.

1st row: P2, work 1st row of panel B across next 12 sts, [p2, work 1st row of panel C across next 8 sts, p2, work 1st row of panel B across next 12 sts] twice, p2.

2nd row: K2, [work 2nd row of panel B, k2, work 2nd row of panel C, k2] twice, work 2nd row of panel B, k2.

These 2 rows set the position of cable panels and form reverse st st between. Continue in pattern as set, **working appropriate rows of panels** and bringing extra sts into pattern, inc 1 st at each end of next 3(9-13) rows, 70(82-90) sts, then every following alt row until there are 140(146-152) sts. Work straight until sleeve measures 46(46-47) cm [18(18-18½) ins] ending with a wrong side row. Cast off.

Finishing and Neckband

Block but do not press. Join left shoulder seam.

Neckband

Using smaller needles and with right side of work facing, pick up and knit 40(41-44) sts across back neck, 17 sts down left front slope, 17(18-19) sts across front neck and 17 sts up right front slope. 91(93-97) sts.

Starting with a 2nd row, work 11 cm [4¼ ins] in k1, p1 rib as given for Back. Slip sts on to a length of yarn.

Join right shoulder seam and ends of neckband. Fold neckband in half to inside and slip-stitch **loosely** in place, allowing for stretch and taking care to catch every stitch.

Fold each sleeve in half lengthways and mark centre of cast off edge. Sew each sleeve to a side edge placing centre at shoulder seam.

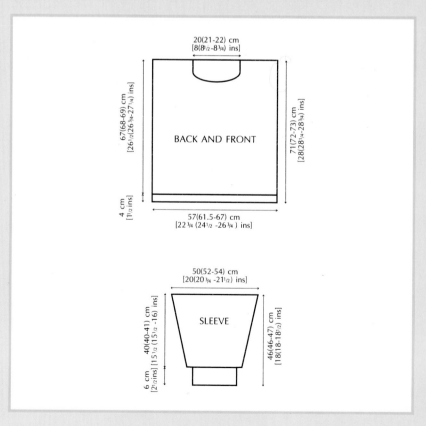

Cable Panels

6th row: P2, k5, p2.

7th row: K2, p5, k2.

8th row: P2, k5, p2.

9th row: T3F, p3, T3B.

10th row: As 4th row.

11th row: P1, T3F, p1, T3B, p1.

12th row: As 2nd row.

Rep these 12 rows.

Chain Cable

Panel of 9 sts on a background of reverse st st.

1st row (right side): P2, T5BP, p2.

2nd row: K2, p2, k1, p2, k2.

3rd row: P1, T3B, p1, T3F, p1.

4th row: K1, p2, k3, p2, k1.

5th row: T3B, p3, T3F.

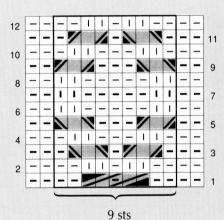

9 sts

Wide Cable Panel

Panel of 20 sts on a background of reverse st st.

1st row (right side): K6, C4B, C4F, k6.

2nd and every alt row: P20.

3rd row: K4, C4B, k4, C4F, k4.

5th row: K2, C4B, k8, C4F, k2.

7th row: C4B, k12, C4F.

8th row: P20.

Rep these 8 rows.

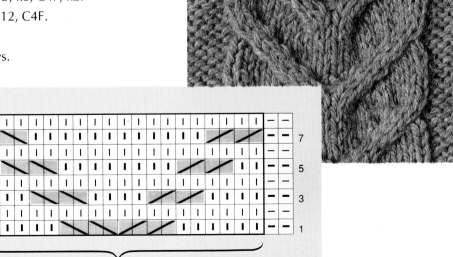

20 sts

Cable Panels

Rope and Lattice Panel

Panel of 26 sts on a background of reverse st st.

1st row (right side): K6, [p4, k6] twice.

2nd row: P6, [k4, p6] twice.

3rd row: C6B, [p4, C6B] twice.

4th row: As 2nd row.

5th to 8th rows: As 1st to 4th rows.

9th row: K3, T5L, p2, k6, p2, T5R, k3.

10th row: [P3, k2] twice, p6, [k2, p3] twice.

11th row: [T5L] twice, k6, [T5R] twice.

12th row: K2, p3, k2, p12, k2, p3, k2.

13th row: P2, T5L, [C6F] twice, T5R, p2.

14th row: K4, p18, k4.

15th row: P4, [C6B] 3 times, p4.

16th row: K4, p18, k4.

17th row: P2, T5R, [C6F] twice, T5L, p2.

18th row: As 12th row.

19th row: [T5R] twice, k6, [T5L] twice.

20th row: As 10th row.

21st row: K3, T5R, p2, k6, p2, T5L, k3.

22nd to 28th rows: As 2nd to 8th rows.

Rep these 28 rows.

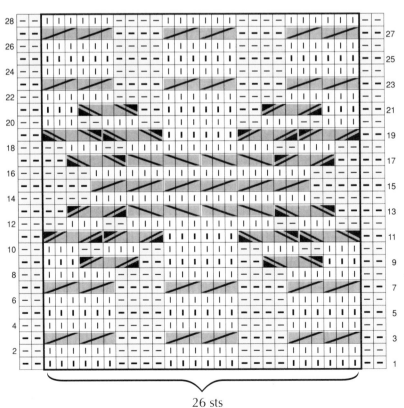

26 sts

Cross and Twist Panel

Panel of 26 sts on a background of reverse st st.

1st row (right side): P1, T4L, T4R, p8, T4L, T4R, p1.

2nd row: K2, p6, k10, p6, k2.

3rd row: P2, C6F, p10, C6F, p2.

4th row: As 2nd row.

5th row: P1, T4R, T4L, p8, T4R, T4L, p1.

6th row: K1, p3, k2, p3, k8, p3, k2, p3, k1.

7th row: T4R, p2, T4L, p6, T4R, p2, T4L.

8th row: P3, k4, p3, k6, p3, k4, p3.

9th row: K3, p4, T4L, p4, T4R, p4, k3.

10th row: P3, k5, p3, k4, p3, k5, p3.

11th row: T4L, p4, T4L, p2, T4R, p4, T4R.

12th row: K1, p3, k5, p3, k2, p3, k5, p3, k1.

13th row: P1, T4L, p4, T4L, T4R, p4, T4R, p1.

14th row: K2, p3, k5, p6, k5, p3, k2.

15th row: P2, T4L, p4, C6B, p4, T4R, p2.

16th row: K3, p3, k4, p6, k4, p3, k3.

17th row: P3, [T4L, p2, T4R] twice, p3.

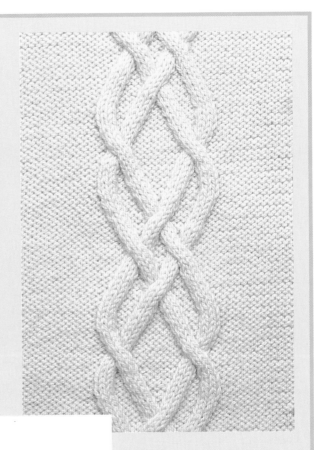

18th row: K4, p3, [k2, p3] 3 times, k4.

19th row: P4, T4L, T4R, p2, T4L, T4R, p4.

20th row: K5, p6, k4, p6, k5.

21st row: P5, C6F, p4, C6F, p5.

22nd row: As 20th row.

23rd row: P4, T4R, T4L, p2, T4R, T4L, p4.

24th row: As 18th row.

25th row: P3, [T4R, p2, T4L] twice, p3.

26th row: As 16th row.

27th row: P2, T4R, p4, C6B, p4, T4L, p2.

28th row: As 14th row.

29th row: P1, T4R, p4, T4R, T4L, p4, T4L, p1.

30th row: As 12th row.

31st row: T4R, p4, T4R, p2, T4L, p4, T4L.

32nd row: As 10th row.

33rd row: K3, p4, T4R, p4, T4L, p4, k3.

34th row: As 8th row.

35th row: T4L, p2, T4R, p6, T4L, p2, T4R.

36th row: As 6th row.

Rep these 36 rows.

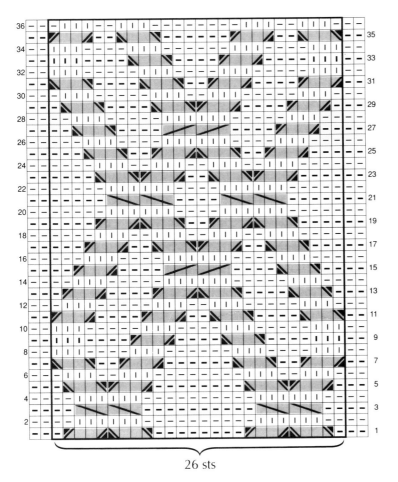

26 sts

Cable Panels

Ornamental Lantern Cable

Panel of 22 sts on a background of reverse st st.

1st row (right side): P9, k4, p9.

2nd row: K9, p4, k9.

3rd row: P7, C4B, C4F, p7.

4th row: K7, p8, k7.

5th row: P5, T4B, C4F, T4F, p5.

6th row: K5, p2, k2, p4, k2, p2, k5.

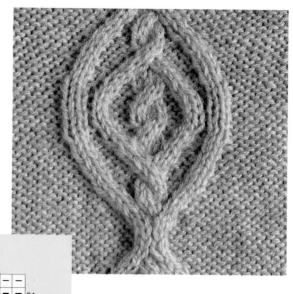

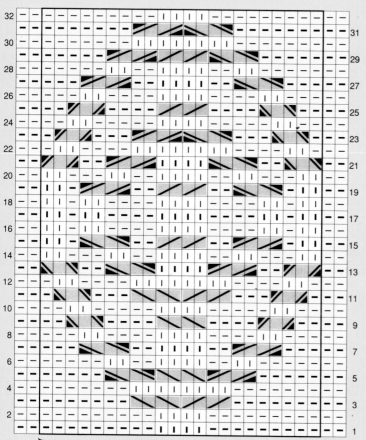

22 sts

13th row: T3B, p2, T4B, k4, T4F, p2, T3F.

14th row: P2, k3, p2, k2, p4, k2, p2, k3, p2.

15th row: K2, p1, T4B, p2, C4B, p2, T4F, p1, k2.

16th row: P2, k1, p2, k4, p4, k4, p2, k1, p2.

17th row: K2, p1, k2, p4, k4, p4, k2, p1, k2.

18th row: As 16th row.

19th row: K2, p1, T4F, p2, C4B, p2, T4B, p1, k2.

20th row: As 14th row.

21st row: T3F, p2, T4F, k4, T4B, p2, T3B.

22nd row: As 12th row.

23rd row: P1, T3F, p3, T4F, T4B, p3, T3B, p1.

24th row: As 10th row.

25th row: P2, T3F, p4, C4B, p4, T3B, p2.

26th row: As 8th row.

27th row: P3, T4F, p2, k4, p2, T4B, p3.

28th row: As 6th row.

7th row: P3, T4B, p2, k4, p2, T4F, p3.

8th row: K3, p2, k4, p4, k4, p2, k3.

9th row: P2, T3B, p4, C4F, p4, T3F, p2.

10th row: K2, p2, k5, p4, k5, p2, k2.

11th row: P1, T3B, p3, C4B, C4F, p3, T3F, p1.

12th row: K1, p2, k4, p8, k4, p2, k1.

29th row: P5, T4F, C4B, T4B, p5.

30th row: As 4th row.

31st row: P7, T4F, T4B, p7.

32nd row: K9, p4, k9.

Rep these 32 rows.

Cable Panels

Serpent Panel

Multiple of 8 sts + 6. The example shown is worked over 22 sts on a background of reverse st st.

Special Abbreviations

T6RP (Twist 6 Right Purl) = slip next 4 sts on to cable needle and hold at back of work, knit next 2 sts from left-hand needle, slip the 2 purl sts from cable needle back to left-hand needle and purl them, then knit 2 sts from cable needle.

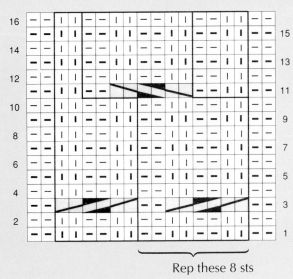

Rep these 8 sts

T6LP (Twist 6 Left Purl) = slip next 4 sts on to cable needle and hold at front of work, knit next 2 sts from left-hand needle, then slip the 2 purl sts from cable needle back on to left-hand needle and purl them, knit 2 sts from cable needle.

1st row (right side): K2, *p2, k2; rep from * to end.

2nd row: P2, *k2, p2; rep from * to end.

3rd row: T6RP, *p2, T6RP; rep from * to end.

4th row: As 2nd row.

5th to 10th rows: Rep 1st and 2nd rows 3 times.

11th row: K2, *p2, T6LP; rep from * to last 4 sts, p2, k2.

12th row: As 2nd row.

13th to 16th rows: Rep 1st and 2nd rows twice.

Rep these 16 rows.

Cable Patterns

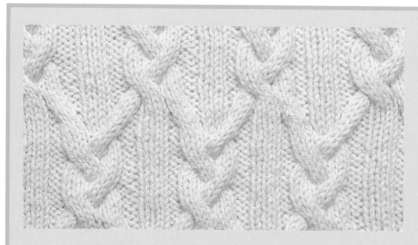

Twisted Cables

Multiple of 18 sts + 19.

1st row (right side): P2, [k3, p3] twice, *k9, p3, k3, p3; rep from * to last 5 sts, k3, p2.

2nd row: K2, [p3, k3] twice, *p9, k3, p3, k3; rep from * to last 5 sts, p3, k2.

3rd row: P2, k3, [p3, k3] twice, *C6F, [p3, k3] twice; rep from * to last 2 sts, p2.

4th row: As 2nd row.

5th and 6th rows: As 1st and 2nd rows.

7th row: P2, [k3, p3] twice, *C6B, [k3, p3] twice; rep from * to last 5 sts, k3, p2.

8th row: As 2nd row.

9th row: P2, T4L, p2, k3, *p2, T4R, k3, T4L, p2, k3; rep from * to last 8 sts, p2, T4R, p2.

10th row: K3, p3, [k2, p3] twice, *[k1, p3] twice, [k2, p3] twice; rep from * to last 3 sts, k3.

11th row: P3, T4L, p1, k3, p1, T4R, *p1, k3, p1, T4L, p1, k3, p1, T4R; rep from * to last 3 sts, p3.

12th row: K4, p3, [k1, p3] twice, *[k2, p3] twice, [k1, p3] twice; rep from * to last 4 sts, k4.

13th row: P4, T4L, k3, T4R, *p2, k3, p2, T4L, k3, T4R; rep from * to last 4 sts, p4.

14th row: K5, p9, *k3, p3, k3, p9; rep from * to last 5 sts, k5.

15th row: P5, k3, C6F, *[p3, k3] twice, C6F; rep from * to last 5 sts, p5.

16th row: As 14th row.

17th row: P5, k9, *p3, k3, p3, k9; rep from * to last 5 sts, p5.

18th row: As 14th row.

19th row: P5, C6B, *[k3, p3] twice, C6B; rep from * to last 8 sts, k3, p5.

20th row: As 14th row.

21st row: As 17th row.

22nd to 28th rows: As 14th to 20th rows.

29th row: P4, T4R, k3, T4L, *p2, k3, p2, T4R, k3, T4L; rep from * to last 4 sts, p4.

30th row: As 12th row.

31st row: P3, T4R, p1, k3, p1, T4L, *p1, k3, p1, T4R, p1, k3, p1, T4L; rep from * to last 3 sts, p3.

32nd row: As 10th row.

33rd row: P2, T4R, p2, k3, p2, T4L, *k3, T4R, p2, k3, p2, T4L; rep from * to last 2 sts, p2.

34th to 40th rows: As 2nd to 8th rows.

Rep these 40 rows.

Rep these 18 sts

Lace and Cable Panels

Lace Cable Pattern

Panel of 6 sts on a background of reverse st st.

1st row (right side): K6.

2nd row: P6.

3rd row: C6B.

4th row: P6.

5th and 6th rows: As 1st and 2nd rows.

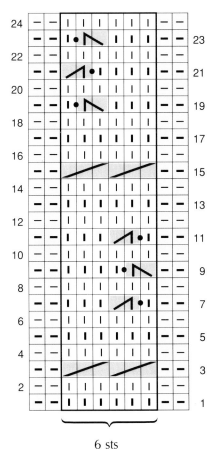

6 sts

7th row: K1, yf, k2tog, k3.

8th row: P6.

9th row: Sl 1, k1, psso, yf, k4.

10th row: P6.

11th and 12th rows: As 7th and 8th rows.

13th to 18th rows: As 1st to 6th rows.

19th row: K3, sl 1, k1, psso, yf, k1.

20th row: P6.

21st row: K4, yf, k2tog.

22nd row: P6.

23rd and 24th rows: As 19th and 20th rows.

Rep these 24 rows.

Lace and Cable Panels

Acorn Leaves

Panel starts with 20 sts and is worked on a background of reverse st st. The number of sts within the panel varies, therefore work between markers.

1st row (right side): P2, yb, sl 1, k1, psso, k1, k2tog, p4, k2, p4, yon, k1, yfrn, p2.

2nd row: K2, p3, k4, p2, k4, p3, k2.

3rd row: P2, yb, sl 1, k2tog, psso, p2, p2tog, k1, M1K, k1, p4, k1, [yf, k1] twice, p2.

4th row: K2, p5, k4, p3, k6.

5th row: P4, p2tog, k1, M1P, k2, p4, k2, yf, k1, yf, k2, p2. (22 sts).

6th row: K2, p7, k4, p2, k1, p1, k5.

7th row: P3, p2tog, k1, M1P, p1, k2, p4, k3, yf, k1, yf, k3, p2. (24 sts).

8th row: K2, p9, k4, p2, k2, p1, k4.

9th row: P2, p2tog, k1, M1P, p2, k2, p4, yb, sl 1, k1, psso, k5, k2tog, p2. (22 sts).

10th row: K2, p7, k4, p2, k3, p1, k3.

11th row: P1, p2tog, k1, M1P, p3, k2, p4, yb, sl 1, k1, psso, k3, k2tog, p2. (20 sts).

12th row: K2, p5, k4, p2, k4, p1, k2.

13th row: P2, yon, k1, yfrn, p4, k2, p4, yb, sl 1, k1, psso, k1, k2tog, p2.

14th row: K2, p3, k4, p2, k4, p3, k2.

15th row: P2, k1, [yf, k1] twice, p4, k1, M1K, k1, p2tog, p2, yb, sl 1, k2tog, psso, p2.

16th row: K6, p3, k4, p5, k2.

17th row: P2, k2, yf, k1, yf, k2, p4, k2, M1P, k1, p2tog, p4. (22 sts).

18th row: K5, p1, k1, p2, k4, p7, k2.

19th row: P2, k3, yf, k1, yf, k3, p4, k2, p1, M1P, k1, p2tog, p3. (24 sts).

20th row: K4, p1, k2, p2, k4, p9, k2.

21st row: P2, yb, sl 1, k1, psso, k5, k2tog, p4, k2, p2, M1P, k1, p2tog, p2. (22 sts).

22nd row: K3, p1, k3, p2, k4, p7, k2.

23rd row: P2, yb, sl 1, k1, psso, k3, k2tog, p4, k2, p3, M1P, k1, p2tog, p1. (20 sts).

24th row: K2, p1, k4, p2, k4, p5, k2.

Rep these 24 rows.

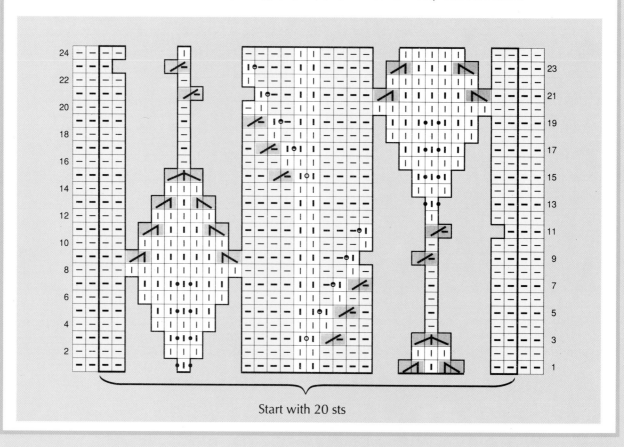

Start with 20 sts

Lace and Cable Patterns

Lattice Pattern

Multiple of 16 sts + 17. The example shown is worked over 33 sts on a background of reverse st st.

Special Abbreviations

T7BP (Twist 7 Back Purl) = slip next 4 sts on to cable needle and hold at back of work, knit next 3 sts from left-hand needle, slip the purl st from cable needle back to left-hand needle and purl it, then knit 3 sts from cable needle.

T7FP (Twist 7 Front Purl) = slip next 4 sts on to cable needle and hold at front of work, knit next 3 sts from left-hand needle, slip the purl st from cable needle back to left-hand needle and purl it, then knit 3 sts from cable needle.

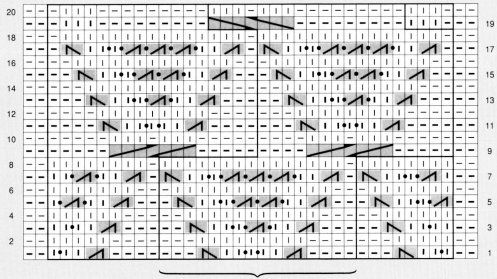

Rep these 16 sts

1st row (right side): K1, *yf, k2, sl 1, k1, psso, p7, k2tog, k2, yf, k1; rep from * to end.

2nd row: P5, *k7, p9; rep from * to last 12 sts, k7, p5.

3rd row: K2, *yf, k2, sl 1, k1, psso, p5, k2tog, k2, yf, k2tog, yf, k1; rep from * to last 15 sts, yf, k2, sl 1, k1, psso, p5, k2tog, k2, yf, k2.

4th row: P6, *k5, p11; rep from * to last 11 sts, k5, p6.

5th row: *K2tog, yf, k1, yf, k2, sl 1, k1, psso, p3, k2tog, k2, yf, k2tog, yf; rep from * to last st, k1.

6th row: P7, *k3, p13; rep from * to last 10 sts, k3, p7.

7th row: K1, k2tog, yf, *k1, yf, k2, sl 1, k1, psso, p1, k2tog, k2, yf, [k2tog, yf] 3 times; rep from * to last 14 sts, k1, yf, k2, sl 1, k1,

psso, p1, k2tog, k2, yf, k2tog, yf, k2.

8th row: P8, *k1, p15; rep from * to last 9 sts, k1, p8.

9th row: P5, *T7BP, p9; rep from * to last 12 sts, T7BP, p5.

10th row: K5, *p3, k1, p3, k9; rep from * to last 12 sts, p3, k1, p3, k5.

11th row: P4, *k2tog, k2, yf, k1, yf, k2, sl 1, k1, psso, p7; rep from * to last 13 sts, k2tog, k2, yf, k1, yf, k2, sl 1, k1, psso, p4.

12th row: K4, *p9, k7; rep from * to last 13 sts, p9, k4.

13th row: P3, *k2tog, k2, yf, k2tog, yf, k1, yf, k2, sl 1, k1, psso, p5; rep from * to last 14 sts, k2tog, k2, yf, k2tog, yf, k1, yf, k2, sl 1, k1, psso, p3.

14th row: K3, *p11, k5; rep from

* to last 14 sts, p11, k3.

15th row: P2, *k2tog, k2, yf, [k2tog, yf] twice, k1, yf, k2, sl 1, k1, psso, p3; rep from * to last 15 sts, k2tog, k2, yf, [k2tog, yf] twice, k1, yf, k2, sl 1, k1, psso, p2.

16th row: K2, *p13, k3; rep from * to last 15 sts, p13, k2.

17th row: P1, *k2tog, k2, yf, [k2tog, yf] 3 times, k1, yf, k2, sl 1, k1, psso, p1; rep from * to end.

18th row: K1, *p15, k1; rep from * to end.

19th row: P1, k3, *p9, T7FP; rep from * to last 13 sts, p9, k3, p1.

20th row: K1, p3, *k9, p3, k1, p3; rep from * to last 13 sts, k9, p3, k1.

Rep these 20 rows.

Lace and Cable Patterns

Wavy Cable Lace

Multiple of 14 sts + 15.

1st row (right side): K1, *yf, k2, p3, p3tog, p3, k2, yf, k1; rep from * to end.

2nd row: P4, *k7, p7; rep from * to last 11 sts, k7, p4.

3rd row: K2, *yf, k2, p2, p3tog, p2, k2, yf, k3; rep from * to last 13 sts, yf, k2, p2, p3tog, p2, k2, yf, k2.

4th row: P5, k5, *p9, k5; rep from * to last 5sts, p5, p5.

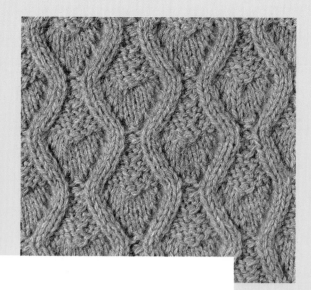

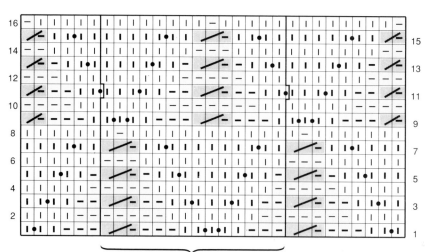

Rep these 14 sts

5th row: K3, *yf, k2, p1, p3tog, p1, k2, yf, k5; rep from * to last 12 sts, yf, k2, p1, p3tog, p1, k2, yf, k3.

6th row: P6, *k3, p11; rep from * to last 9 sts, k3, p6.

7th row: K4, *yf, k2, p3tog, k2, yf, k7; rep from * to last 11 sts, yf, k2, p3tog, k2, yf, k4.

8th row: P7, *k1, p13; rep from * to last 8 sts, k1, p7.

9th row: P2tog, *p3, k2, yf, k1, yf, k2, p3, p3tog; rep from * to last 13 sts, p3, k2, yf, k1, yf, k2, p3, p2tog.

10th row: K4, *p7, k7; rep from * to last 11 sts, p7, k4.

11th row: P2tog, *p2, k2, yf, k3, yf, k2, p2, p3tog; rep from * to last 13 sts, p2, k2, yf, k3, yf, k2, p2, p2tog.

12th row: K3, *p9, k5; rep from * to last 12 sts, p9, k3.

13th row: P2tog, *p1, k2, yf, k5, yf, k2, p1, p3tog; rep from * to last 13 sts, p1, k2, yf, k5, yf, k2, p1, p2tog.

14th row: K2, *p11, k3; rep from * to last 13 sts, p11, k2.

15th row: P2tog, *k2, yf, k7, yf, k2, p3tog; rep from * to last 13 sts, k2, yf, k7, yf, k2, p2tog.

16th row: K1, *p13, k1; rep from * to end.

Rep these 16 rows.